1 Corinthians

1 CORINTHIANS: SEARCHING THE DEPTHS OF GOD

1 Corinthians

978-1-5018-9143-4
978-1-5018-9144-1 eBook

1 Corinthians DVD

978-1-5018-9147-2

1 Corinthians Leader Guide

978-1-5018-9145-8
978-1-5018-9146-5 eBook

ALSO BY JAIME CLARK-SOLES FROM ABINGDON PRESS

The CEB Women's Bible (co-editor)

Covenant Bible Study (co-author)

Disciple Bible Study (contributor)

1 CORINTHIANS

Searching the Depths of God

Jaime Clark-Soles

Abingdon Press / Nashville

1 CORINTHIANS
SEARCHING THE DEPTHS OF GOD

Library of Congress Control Number: 2020950905

978-1-5018-9143-4

21 22 23 24 25 26 27 28 29 30—10 9 8 7 6 5 4 3 2 1
MANUFACTURED IN THE UNITED STATES OF AMERICA

To my students,
who grant me the joy of reading Scripture
in community.

CONTENTS

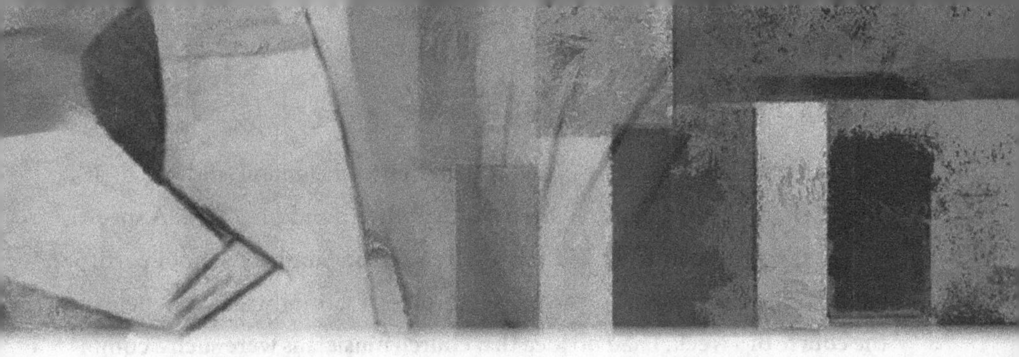

Acknowledgments

Two years ago this month, I sat down to breakfast with one Maria Mayo, editor at Abingdon Press. I'm not a morning person and I warned her about that. I also let her know that though I was glad to meet with her (since I could tell from our initial exchange that she's someone I'd like to know), there's no way I could agree to write a book just then. By the end of breakfast, we decided that I would, in fact, write a book and that it would be on 1 Corinthians. In my defense, she gave me a centurion finger puppet as a gift and made writing such a book sound fun. That's Maria! I am grateful for her editorial prowess and her ability to bring out what an author is passionate about and then turn them loose to talk about that in their own way (while also noting where it might be best to "rein it in" a bit). Not only did I have an excellent editor, but I also made a new friend.

I thank God regularly for my friend, biblical studies colleague, and writing accountability partner Dr. Anathea Portier-Young, who teaches Old Testament/Hebrew Bible. I can't imagine the writing process without her.

April Simpson, who is completing her PhD in New Testament, worked as my research assistant for the bulk of the time I wrote this book. She helped me think through its contents and plan and vetted my arguments in the early chapters. She was succeeded by Kelsey Spinnato, who is completing her PhD in Old Testament/Hebrew Bible. Kelsey's editing and insights have been invaluable.

I thank Lindsay Blake Bruehl for her encouragement and input. It's good to have a "spicy Baptist" on speed-dial when pondering Paul! A special thanks goes to Leah King and the Church Music Summer School participants who, many years ago, journeyed through 1 Corinthians with me over the course of a week. I had no idea that church musicians were such a combination of fun, clever, creative, and inspiring. They have you belly-laughing one minute and then move you to tears the next by drawing you right into the heart of God with their music and their very selves.

As always, my family sustains me and invariably finds themselves subjected to whatever I'm writing on in any given period. My husband, Thad, has been at this with me for over thirty years now. Both of my children, Chloe and Caleb, are engaging conversation partners, so I love discussing big ideas with them. A special thanks goes to Caleb and Monique for the conversation about hair, weaves, and Hair Love as it relates to 1 Corinthians 11.

I owe thanks both for the Perkins Scholarly Outreach grant that I was awarded in support of this book and for the Sam Taylor Fellowship.

Finally, I cannot thank enough my friends and colleagues who agreed to appear in the videos that accompany this book: Rev. Dr. George Mason; Rev. Ellen Dittman; Rev. Ray Jordan; Rev. Dr. Baranda Fermin; Rev. Mireya Martinez; and Rev. Katie Montgomery Mears, who also wrote the Leader Guide that accompanies this book. I chose well. Each of these people loves Scripture as much as I do and continues to teach me how to interpret it in life-giving ways for everybody. Every. Body. They stimulate my thinking and they show me what grace looks like by the way they live. Like Paul, they continually search the depths of God and, in turn, invite us to do the same.

I give thanks to God for the gift of reading and studying Scripture in community. I pray that God blesses your study of 1 Corinthians and that you encounter the grace of Christ as you go.

Jaime Clark-Soles
November 2020

INTRODUCTION

Unlikely Christians: Paul, the Corinthians, Me—and You?

"Last of all, as to one untimely born, he appeared also to me" (1 Corinthians 15:8). I love this line from one of Christianity's most compelling figures—Paul—and I relate. I didn't grow up in church. Well, I mean, my parents had a stint soon after my sister was born such that we were both baptized in matching dresses when I was about seven (one of the *very* few pictures of me in a dress, and not at *all* voluntary!), but that went south pretty quickly as my parents were made to feel too "worldly" by the Daughters of Ruth church group.

Then there was Father James Patrick Seamus O'Kielty (he was Irish, in case you're wondering), the Catholic priest of families stationed in Gaeta, Italy, as was my family most of my teenage years. In the overseas military, you don't have Baptist, Methodist, Church of God in Christ, Presbyterian, and so forth. You have Catholic and Protestant, and you meet in the space in the Community Center (at different appointed times) that doubles as a gym. My best friend Kimmy Lou, also a military brat, was Catholic. Every once in a while, I was able to arrange a sleepover at Kimmy Lou's house, and when I spent the night at her house, I went to Catholic church with her the next day. There in that room with linoleum tile and makeshift everything, I encountered the divine in a mysterious, luminous way that remains hard to describe, but that affected my life profoundly.

I was thirteen. Father O'Kielty led worship, and I tried to follow when to kneel, when to sit, when to rise, and what to say when. Then there was this moment that is emblazoned on my brain; he turned away from us and addressed God in a way that involved Latin and the elements and beauty and grandeur and thin space and majesty. In that moment the ratty room became for me the kind of holy space that only people like Teresa of Avila have ever come close to describing effectively: a crystal palace of immense beauty and spaciousness (room for *all*) and grace and rest. It was a moment that shaped my life to come, even if I didn't know that consciously right then. A few days later we were at the commissary, and the same Father O'Kielty, ahead of my family in the line, joked (yes, a clergyperson with a robust sense of humor) with those behind him, "I'm taking up an offering to pay for my groceries." Wow. A person who had one foot on earth and one in heaven. Able to connect us regular folks with the ineffable divine so that we are speechless and filled with nothing but wonder and gratitude one minute and laughing about how real the grocery bill is the next.

Partway through my senior year of high school, my dad was stationed first in Pensacola, Florida, for two months and then in Orlando. Having lived out of the country from ages ten to seventeen, I now found myself living on a US Navy base where I very occasionally went to a Protestant service on my own. I recall one of them moved me enough to ask the preacher for a copy of the sermon, which he provided. I still have it.

In college I majored in philosophy and minored in Russian studies. In such a small school, philosophy and religion overlapped (as they had for all preceding centuries until the late twentieth). There, for the first time, I encountered in my professors intellectual Christians—Christians who were not afraid of knowledge of all sorts, and in fact *relished* it. None of this, "You know, Jaime, you can be so open-minded that your brains fall out." Or, "Oh, you're going to seminary? Do you mean 'cemetery,' where they *kill* your faith?"

I recall specifically a course I took on existentialism for my philosophy degree. We had just read Elie Wiesel's *The Trial of God*. I was twenty years old and had, by then, also read *Night* by Wiesel as well as Victor Frankl's *Man's Search for Meaning*. As I listened to some of my Christian classmates vigorously protest the notion of questioning God (which I do not judge them for), I found myself in a strange position. On the one hand, I was a Christian, having made that sincere, deliberate choice in January 1986 at a camp that, oddly, belonged to a church that later I would serve. On the other hand, I felt far more connection with the complaints of the Jew Elie Wiesel, who was calling God to account, than I did with my fellow Christians who, it seemed to me, were satisfied to passively accept the Holocaust, all holocausts, really, as "God's will."

In that moment, even though I couldn't quote 1 Corinthians 15:8 yet, I felt that I, too, was "untimely born" when it comes to the Christian faith. If our God could not withstand being "put on trial" by thinking, feeling, aching, longing-for-meaning-and-justice-and-wholeness finite human beings (go read the Lament Psalms), then count me out. I have no interest in, respect for, or commitment to such a fragile God. Because not only was I a philosophy major, but I was also doing equal work in Russian studies. That means I read very early on in my life the best presentation of the issue of theodicy in all of literature: the chapters "Rebellion" and "The Grand Inquisitor" in *The Brothers Karamazov*. Like Ivan Karamazov, I had protests about where and how God is acting in the world, with precious little children suffering and dying. Some things were not adding up for me: Is God omnipotent (all powerful) but malevolent (does not will the good)? Or is God benevolent (wills what is good) but impotent (unable to enact God's will)? Ivan concisely and poignantly voiced my very concerns. But Dostoevsky

Ask yourself at every turn: "If what Paul is saying here is true, what would it mean for me, my community, our world? Is this an ethic that, were I to commit to it, could mean abundant life and flourishing for me and all of God's creation?"

was ready for me in the form of not just the Grand Inquisitor (a Catholic Cardinal executing the Inquisition), and not just Alyosha Karamazov (a priest), but also Jesus himself.

And so Jesus captivated me and invited me into even bigger questions and quests for truth. When I ask my questions, I hear Jesus say, "Right? And if that isn't tricky enough, have you thought about *this* conundrum?" I have spent decades shining light in all the corners and nooks and crannies of the faith asking, "Wait, what about *this*?" and I won't stop this side of the grave as it's my nature. But I will say that now I'm at an age and stage where I've let go of some of the earnestness and need to know details, and I've relaxed more into the curiosity and mystery and assurance that God is God. The one who "keeps Israel / will neither slumber nor sleep" (Psalm 121:4)—despite how things might appear—so I can. So now I invite others into what I call "thought experiments" related to Scripture and faith. Try the ideas on for size—you don't have to commit. Ask yourself at every turn: "If what Paul is saying here is true, what would it mean for me, my community, our world? Is this an ethic that, were I to commit to it, could mean abundant life and flourishing for me and all of God's creation?"

You could say I didn't grow up in church, or you could say I experimented. I can tell you that nobody saw it coming that I'd end up an ordained Baptist minister teaching the Bible in a seminary. On the night of my ordination, my mom asked in a genuinely curious, good, not snarky way, "How did this happen?" Trust me, it's a great question, and I continue to ask it. I think Paul's mom would ask the same question.

Paul was most certainly an unlikely Christian—in fact, he *persecuted* Christians right up until he became one. And the Corinthians were unlikely Christians. And honestly, even once they became Christians, Paul made it clear they were baby Christians—needing a mother's milk—who required lots of instruction, invitation, practice, and correction along the way. Paul himself considered the Christian life an ongoing process of "becoming" (1 Corinthians 13:12; compare Philippians 3:12-14) and warned us all away from anyone who claimed to have "arrived" already (there were a bunch of such folks in Corinth; probably at least as many as we have in our world today; compare 1 Corinthians 4:8, noting Paul's heavy sarcasm).

As I write, I'm drinking coffee from a mug I got from an alum's church that says, "What's your story?" And that's the question I have for you. Whether you were born in the church and don't remember a time apart from it or have a more textured history like me, one untimely born, know that we are all right on time to embrace our gifts and destiny as they relate to the work of God, defined as love.

Now, you may ask, "What does *my* personal story have to do with anything, especially compared to someone as famous as Paul?" And I (and Paul) would respond by insisting that your story is crucial to the whole arc of the narrative of human history known as God-with-Us (Immanuel). Paul was effective in his world—except for all the times he wasn't—*precisely* as Paul, the one who went from persecuting Christians to becoming one to spending his life inviting others in until he died from it and for it. I think it's fascinating the number of times Paul refers to his own life, his own story, as he beckons others into faith. I love that he has come to terms with his own story and accepted it, allowing it to be part of his own way of relating to others like and unlike him.

Paul does not mess with false humility. He owns his achievements and authority without apology; he also isn't enslaved to his ego. He takes an honest look at himself, asks what he can do to be useful to God's purposes in his own context, then does the best he can with what he's got. Turns out that he runs into trouble and conflict at every turn. But he is able to stay the course because he is self-aware and determined to serve others humbly, if forcefully and energetically, given his personality type. We, too, are called to honest self-assessment, a sense of gratitude and humor for all that we are and all that we can be, as we give the world the best we've got here and now.

Whatever your story, it is important. We all bring something to the table, and what a wonderful mix we are! In describing American society, Eboo Patel, founder of Interfaith Youth Core and an Ismaili Muslim, invokes the image of a huge "potluck," where everyone brings "something to the big, open table that welcomes different contributions." He prefers this over the notion of a "melting pot," which seeks to eliminate distinctiveness.[1] I invite us as Christians to adopt this same image of a potluck. As we come to the larger community, we each bring our gifts and stories. We can only tell the gospel story from our perspective, from the way our story intersects with The Story. Whether you "tell it slant," or tell it straight, or something in between, tell it.[2] First Corinthians can help.

The Shape of This Book

I consider 1 Corinthians "the church's book." I suggest that everyone considering joining a church be required to read it and then asked: "Are you ready to be part of this?" If I asked you to make a list of issues in your church, I think you'd be hard-pressed to top the church in Corinth. Community is simultaneously crucial and complicated. Name a subject about participating in community that *doesn't* come up in 1 Corinthians. Factions, sexual ethics, gender issues, money issues, class hierarchies, theological questions, how to conduct worship, and leadership questions—Paul covers it all in this letter.

If I asked you to make a list of issues in your church, I think you'd be hard-pressed to top the church in Corinth. Community is simultaneously crucial and complicated. Name a subject about participating in community that doesn't come up in 1 Corinthians.

And then there are the ways this letter speaks into our personal, individual lives. Paul is a person with an array of experiences and emotions. Tender and outrageous and passionate and reflective and learned. Paul struggles, he exults, he rejoices, he laments, he theologizes, he praises, he questions, all the while experiencing a "thorn in the flesh." Don't we? Where is God in the midst of all of this? How does Jesus tend to us, challenge us, and save us through it all? How can we discern our own spiritual gifts and God-given purpose in this life? What about death and afterlife?

First Corinthians (and its companion, 2 Corinthians) will make you laugh, cry, and lose your breath for the wonder of it all. If allowed, it teaches us a logic [*logos*] that depends on *love*, that word that is so overused and underperformed. It invites us to be fierce for the gospel and tender with people. To be against systems of domination but compassionate toward those caught up in them (which is all of us, in the end).

It's just all in there. Paul the complicated, layered apostle writes to a group of people who are trying some wild new social experiment known as a Christian community. A word about my use of *Christian* when talking about Paul and his ministry. We don't know when Paul was born, but we deduce he died between 62 and 67 CE. In this book I will refer to Paul as a Christian, but with two caveats. First, during Paul's own lifetime Christianity was a developing movement representing one form of Judaism. The move from a primarily Jewish to a primarily Gentile phenomenon took decades, with Paul playing a large role in evangelizing Gentiles. There is no clear date at which "Christianity" and "Judaism" clearly severed, though the destruction of the Jewish temple in 70 CE helped solidify the divergence. Second, even after becoming a Christ follower and "apostle to the Gentiles," Paul identified as a Jew to his dying day (see, for example, Romans 9:3. For more on this topic, I recommend Pamela Eisenbaum's *Paul Was Not a Christian*).

The Corinthians are a substantial mess, a heap of trouble, yet Paul calls them saints. He, of all people, should know what it's like to miss the point, to be "all-in" and only later learn it was for the wrong cause. To never quite "fit in" anywhere, given his hybrid self, while being able to change people everywhere, given his hybrid self (consult 1 Corinthians 9:19-23). Simply stated, 1 Corinthians is one of the most gripping books in the Bible. Whether you read it together as a community or as an individual who is part of a religious community (sorry, Paul doesn't envision anyone being a Christian all alone) and part of a larger world of religious pluralism and governmental forces and societal trends and values, your study will be rewarded.

Come along with me as we make forays into the text, choosing to highlight some of the most prominent aspects of the letter. We'll explore what Paul's overarching purpose was in writing to the Corinthians (hint: they weren't getting along!), what Paul had to say about relationships and how his expectation about Jesus's return shaped his ethics, what freedom meant to Paul, how he thought believers should gather and share their gifts, and his understanding of bodies in present sufferings and future redemption. Through it all, I hope to introduce you to resources, inspire you to study more deeply Paul's extended correspondence with the Corinthians, and make you want to study other Pauline texts. Most of all, I hope you encounter God and Jesus and the Holy Spirit afresh in ways that remind you that you are God's beloved, called to love:

> *If I have prophetic powers, and understand* all *mysteries and* all *knowledge, and if I have* all *faith, so as to remove mountains, but do not have love, I am nothing.*
>
> *1 Corinthians 13:2, emphasis added*

> *Now faith, hope, and love abide, these three; and the greatest of these is love.*
>
> *1 Corinthians 13:13*

Indeed.

CHAPTER 1

CAN'T WE ALL JUST GET ALONG?

CORINTH

Paul established house churches in Corinth around 50 CE. According to 1 Corinthians 5:9 he had also written another letter, which scholars refer to as "the lost letter." So, really, our "1 Corinthians" is at least his *second* letter, written around 54 CE. Most scholars find in our 2 Corinthians multiple letters, perhaps including the "lost letter" of 1 Corinthians 5:9, which some believe is found in 2 Corinthians 6:14–7:1. Long story short, Paul made two visits and wrote four letters to this church that he loved so very dearly. The Corinthians caused him to feel a wide array of emotions, from tears of pain, to anger, to tenderness and, most of all, love. In the middle of a gut-wrenching exchange where he is addressing the conflict between him and them, he declares: "I will most gladly spend and be spent for you" (2 Corinthians 12:15).

I can't imagine a more beautiful or concise statement of what Christian love entails. First Corinthians 12:2 indicates that the recipients of the letter were Gentiles (that is, not Jews), though surely there was a synagogue in Corinth. In fact, when you visit the ancient site of Corinth today, you will see an inscription that suggests as much, since part of the phrase "synagogue of the Hebrews" is etched on it. Corinth was quite an important city in Paul's time. Although it had been destroyed in 146 BCE, in 44 BCE Julius Caesar established it as a Roman colony. Then, in 27 BCE, it became the capital of the whole region of Achaia (refer to a map of the Mediterranean world in your study Bible). Corinth was a multicultural, multiethnic, multilingual, multireligious place, not unlike our own.

Why Did Paul Write the Letter?

Why did Paul write 1 Corinthians? There are clues in the text. First, he received an oral report from "Chloe's people" (1:11). In Paul's time Christians met in house churches, not dedicated buildings. Early Christianity was unusual in that people of different economic strata gathered together in community; so, the Christians with financial resources hosted the church in their homes. Chloe likely was a woman of her own means (no male is mentioned) who led a church in her home. Incidentally, I named my daughter after this strong woman (not after a perfume or a Kardashian, thank you very much). Women in leadership are absolutely typical for Paul.

Second, the Corinthians wrote him a letter asking him to address issues occurring in their own community. How do we know? By the phrase "Now concerning" [*peri de*]; see, for example, 1 Corinthians 7:1; 7:25; 8:1; 12:1; 16:1. Every time you encounter this phrase it means that Paul has moved on to a new topic about which the Corinthians consulted him. In other words, 1 Corinthians is an "occasional letter," which is to say Paul wrote it to a specific congregation in a specific historical context that was experiencing specific problems (that other congregations may or may not have been experiencing). He didn't set out to write a systematic theology, like John Calvin or Karl Barth did, in which he addresses all topics for all time. Nor did he imagine he was writing something that would later become Scripture. In fact, Paul himself thought that the world was ending very soon. As it turns out, the world didn't end, and such occasional letters did become part of Scripture, in large part because our Christian ancestors decided that

> ***1 Corinthians is an "occasional letter," which is to say Paul wrote it to a specific congregation in a specific historical context that was experiencing specific problems.***

there was enough in them that applied to other churches in different times and places. Sure, we Christians no longer divide the world into such hierarchical, binary categories as Jew and Gentile or slave and master, nor do we lose sleep about eating or avoiding meat sacrificed to idols. But we definitely have our own binaries, hierarchies, and conundrums over how much and in what ways a Christian should participate in civil religion, how we are to use our freedom in Christ, and how we treat fellow Christians who may be different from us in worldview. We'll unpack that when we discuss 1 Corinthians 8–10.

Third, in 1 Corinthians 16:17, we learn that Stephanas, Fortunatus, and Achaicus have come from Corinth in person to meet with Paul about the problems. It's important to know that, thanks to the Roman road system, early Christians were able to travel widely and even developed a system of hospitality including hotels and hospitals along the way. This aided the spread of the gospel. It allowed Paul to travel extensively and establish churches; as Frederick Buechner puts it, "He planted churches the way Johnny Appleseed planted trees."[1] Sometimes Paul is even referred to as "the second founder of Christianity"—though we should note that he did not establish the churches in Rome, Alexandria, or Antioch, three crucial centers of early Christianity.

The Structure of the Letter

When we write letters, we follow conventions. Imagine you are the chair of the youth department at your church and are writing a fundraising letter to raise money for the youth ministry. How would you start off? Dear So-and-So (whether you know them or not, you will call them "Dear" out of convention). You then state your name and what office or position you are writing from, such that the recipient should listen to you. Then you thank them for their generosity or other virtues you have seen them display in the past that give you the confidence to believe that they will respond to the observations, information, and request you are about to make. Only after building the connection will you move to "the ask." You write the body of the letter in the conventional form of your society: paragraphs. You end with a kind word and a conventional closing (Sincerely, Best Wishes, Blessings) and sign your name.

Paul's letters follow the letter-writing conventions of his own day. They open with a greeting from the sender(s)—in this case Paul and Sosthenes—to the church(es) in question. He wishes them grace and peace and then moves into what scholars identify as the thanksgiving period of a Pauline letter, which has three functions. First, it gives thanks; the Greek word is *eucharistō* and, as you can see, we get the word "Eucharist" from it. Second, it builds bonds across the distance, just as we do when we write a letter to a friend. Third, it signals the main points of the letter.

In 1 Corinthians 1:4-9, the thanksgiving portion of this letter, what major themes do we find foreshadowed? For one, Paul mentions spiritual gifts. How are spiritual gifts functioning in Corinth? "You are not lacking in any spiritual gift," he says (1:7), but he's getting ready to admonish them on that topic because they are actually using their gifts for their own egos, not for gracing the world. And what about "In every way you have been enriched in him, in speech and knowledge of every kind" (1:5)? Paul launches right into that in chapter 1 and he confronts them because their use of knowledge, far from enlightening and illuminating and improving the community, just makes them full of themselves. Their use of knowledge does not serve the cause of love. "Knowledge puffs up, but love builds up" (8:1).

A caveat is in order here. Paul never eschews the importance of knowledge and learning and reason; in fact, he commands Christians to engage in the life of the mind (Romans 12:2), and he himself is extremely educated. There's not an anti-intellectual bone in his body. Any knowledge, training, or skill can be used for good or ill, can build up or destroy, can serve or enslave others. We are invited to use our powers for good, for God.

After the thanksgiving, Paul's letters include a body, which contains the main business of the letter, followed by a closing, which includes personal greetings similar to those we might include in the opening of a friendly letter today. In 1 Corinthians, Paul spends the body of the letter addressing various issues and concerns. He concludes with a little flair—a kind of Alfred Hitchcock cameo appearance or a John Hancock move: "I, Paul, write this greeting with my own hand" (unlike the rest of the letter, that is; 16:21). He then pronounces a curse on some people and commands the recipients to kiss each other, both elements I plan to leave in the first century. He ends on love "in Christ Jesus" (16:24). And why wouldn't he? If this letter is about anything, it's about the Logic of Love, Jesus-style.

The Logic of the Cross: Christ's Body in Corinth (1 Corinthians 1:18-25)

The "logic of the cross," as Paul calls it: "For on the one hand, the logic of the cross [*ho logos o tou staurou*] is foolishness to the ones who are in the process of perishing; but on the other hand, to the ones who are in the process of being healed/saved, it is the wisdom of God" (1 Corinthians 1:18, my translation). I'm sorry that translations empty the force of the phrase *logos tou staurou* with something like "the message about the cross" (NRSV). We get the word "logic" from *logos.* What's at stake for Paul here is that we live with intention, on purpose, logically—not just with *any* intention or purpose or logic, but with that which derives from the values on

What's at stake for Paul here is that we live with intention, on purpose, logically—not just with* any *intention or purpose or logic, but with that which derives from the values on display in the life, death, and resurrection of Jesus. It's the Logic of Love.

display in the life, death, and resurrection of Jesus. It's the Logic of Love, of reconciliation with God and one another and all of creation.

This Logic of the Cross clashes strongly with other logics we are exposed to daily, which is why Paul uses the rhetorical technique of *contrast* so often in an effort to get our attention and clarify the choices before us. He contrasts not only destruction and healing, but also foolishness and wisdom. And this leads to another technique he relies on heavily: *irony*. For Paul, the Christian life of discipleship is nothing if not ironic. I couldn't agree more. Things are not as they appear. What seems wise to the world (looking out for number one; acting as though your choices don't affect others; the one who dies with the most toys wins) is actually foolishness by God's standards. What seems foolish to the world (compassion and connection; regarding each person as equally valuable regardless of social status; following a crucified Messiah) is wisdom in God's estimation.

The Corinthians have a host of issues in their community, but there's one solution to them all: adopt the Logic of the Cross. In the pages ahead, we'll unpack what that looks like on the ground in concrete practical situations. For now, it's important to highlight several points.

First, Paul presents the cross as the paradigm of power (again, irony). He contrasts and defines (or we might say "redefines") power and weakness. Crucifying Jesus of Nazareth was nothing unusual for the Roman soldiers who went to work that day—just another day at the office. By the world's logic, Rome was the paragon of power that day and Jesus the epitome of weakness; Caesar won. The Logic of the Cross says otherwise. The gospel declares not only that Caesar (or any earthly leader) is not God (though many will try to convince us otherwise), but also that God's version of power prevails when all is said and done.

Far from this being a mere doctrinal belief for Paul, Paul had his own personal experience of the ironic redefinition of power and weakness. He, too, experienced bodily pain, disfigurement, even a "thorn in the flesh" (most likely a physical impairment) for which he was maligned. He writes to the Corinthians about it, again contrasting and redefining power and weakness for them through the words of God: "Three times I appealed to the Lord about this, that it would leave me, but he said to me, 'My grace is sufficient for you, for power is made perfect in weakness.' So, I will boast all the more gladly of my weaknesses, so that the power of Christ may dwell in me. Therefore I am content with weaknesses, insults, hardships, persecutions, and calamities for the sake of Christ; for whenever I am weak, then I am strong" (2 Corinthians 12:8–10).

Second, the cross contrasts and redefines wisdom and foolishness. Third, the cross is the point of unity for Christians. It provides their identity and dictates their morality. It is the central metaphor of the Christian faith for Paul. Where the cross is effective, love [*agapē*] and fellowship [*koinonia*] reign. Read chapter 13 of 1 Corinthians, and you'll get what I mean.

Challenges: Infighting and Spiritual Immaturity (1 Corinthians 1–2)

Divisions, bickering, cliques, religious know-it-alls. Paul tackles these issues from the start because they underlie all of the other problems in some way or another. Reread 1 Corinthians 1:10-17. Here, Paul addresses "divisions" and "quarrels" among the Corinthians. Far from having the tone of a

Model UN debate in which people disagree respectfully and maturely based upon genuinely good and reasoned arguments, Paul depicts his Corinthian siblings more in terms of junior high cliques dedicated to their favorite Instagram influencer of the moment: "What I mean is that each of you says, 'I belong to Paul,' or 'I belong to Apollos,' or 'I belong to Cephas,' or 'I belong to Christ'" (1:12). I have to admit that the last faction really went for it. It reminds me of a church I used to pass by every day driving my kids to school called the "True Christian Church." Okay, you win.

Solution: Unity in Christ (Not Uniformity)

The solution is unity and humility, both of which are contained in the Logic of the Cross. When we start talking about "unity" and "humility," some may feel unsure how to apply these heady theoretical, churchy words. Some may fear that they call for a lot of work with potentially little payoff. Some may fear that their own needs and desires will get eclipsed or dismissed. Some may even understand these concepts as a call to become a doormat for someone else.

Such is the rhetoric of the ego (from the Greek word *egō*, meaning I), or what Paul often refers to as "the flesh" (which we'll define here as the "false self"). If you've done anything with the Enneagram or Richard Rohr, that definition is probably familiar. My PhD is in New Testament, not psychology, so I'll stay in my lane here and tell you with certainty that Paul never became a doormat or stopped having strong convictions. What he discovered was the truth of Jesus's ironic words about losing in order to gain, dying in order to live. This is a man who was the top of his class at the best school, winning every medal, crushing it left and right.

> *I, too, have reason for confidence in the flesh.*
>
> *If anyone else has reason to be confident in the flesh, I have more:*

> *circumcised on the eighth day, a member of the people of Israel, of the tribe of Benjamin, a Hebrew born of Hebrews; as to the law, a Pharisee; as to zeal, a persecutor of the church; as to righteousness under the law, blameless.*
>
> *Yet whatever gains I had, these I have come to regard as loss because of Christ. More than that, I regard everything as loss because of the surpassing value of knowing Christ Jesus my Lord. For his sake I have suffered the loss of all things, and I regard them as rubbish, in order that I may gain Christ and be found in him.*
>
> *Philippians 3:4-9*

Over and over, in a variety of ways, Paul tries to get at these points:

1. We all have spiritual gifts. Literally, we are all "God's gift to the world." The very reason God gave us gifts is to contribute to the flourishing of all God's creation.
2. Some people are stuck in shame and don't recognize that they are God's gift. They play small and hide and need to be encouraged to step up to the plate and shine their light. If you want sin language, this could be called "the sin of hiding." They might benefit from reading Marianne Williamson's words:

   > 'Our deepest fear is not that we are inadequate. Our deepest fear is that we are powerful beyond measure. It is our light, not our darkness, that most frightens us.' We ask ourselves, Who am I to be brilliant, gorgeous, talented, fabulous? Actually, who are you *not* to be? You are a child of God. Your playing small doesn't serve the world. There's nothing enlightened about shrinking so that other people won't feel insecure around you. We are all meant to shine, as children do. We were born to make manifest the glory of God that is within us. It's not just in some of us; it's in everyone. And as we let our own light shine, we unconsciously

give other people permission to do the same. As we're liberated from our own fear, our presence automatically liberates others.[2]

3. Other people struggle with the opposite—they could regale you for hours with proof that they are God's gift. They are tempted to be arrogant and self-centered and to use their gifts for self-promotion. They mistakenly imagine that their success is to be credited to them alone or that it as a joint effort between them and the God who so especially extra-gifted them. They balk at the idea that anyone else or even a community or a society contributed to their success. This could be called "the sin of pride." They might benefit from reading, well, 1 Corinthians.
4. As counterintuitive, or ironic, as it might feel to many of us, unity and humility do not diminish us; rather, they liberate us. When we understand that we are, by God's design, connected to all God's creation, it means that together, we are more than we could be on our own. When we realize that, by God's design, we are each gifted in certain ways (and not in others), we can relax into that fact without envying someone else or pretending to be something we aren't. We are honest—but not arrogant—about our gifts and glad to name and appreciate those we find in others. That's unity and humility.

The Corinthians can't see the forest for the trees. What would it be like if they could set aside their bickering on the ground and view reality from God's perspective ("on earth as it is in heaven," in Jesus's words)? They would get the big picture. Notice that Paul does not capitalize on the loyalty of the "Paul faction" to one-up his colleagues or promote himself. Quite the opposite—he redirects their loyalty away from him and to Christ, as all good Christian leaders do in all times and places. If possible, read it out loud to get the full effect, especially verse 16, which makes me smile with the interjected "aside" that appears in parentheses (you, my reader, can probably already deduce that I'm a fan of asides). It really is like Paul himself is there with them:

> *Has Christ been divided? Was Paul crucified for you? Or were you baptized in the name of Paul? I thank God that I baptized none of you except Crispus and Gaius, so that no one can say that you were baptized in my name. (I did baptize also the household of Stephanas; beyond that, I do not know whether I baptized anyone else.) For Christ did not send me to baptize but to proclaim the gospel, and not with eloquent wisdom, so that the cross of Christ might not be emptied of its power.*
>
> *1 Corinthians 1:13-17*

I note two points regarding unity in 1 Corinthians 1–4. First, Paul models cooperation instead of competition, noting that he and the other leaders cooperate in order to build something grand, a Christian community. Here's part of what he says:

> *What then is Apollos? What is Paul? Servants through whom you came to believe, as the Lord assigned to each. I planted, Apollos watered, but God gave the growth. So neither the one who plants nor the one who waters is anything, but only God who gives the growth. The one who plants and the one who waters have a common purpose, and each will receive wages according to the labor of each. For we are God's servants, working together; you [plural] are God's field, God's building.*
>
> *1 Corinthians 3:5-9*

The unity is found in the "working together" toward the "common purpose" of growing and building a community. As Paul will make clear in 1 Corinthians 13, that community is to be marked by the greatest virtue of all: not hope, and, surprisingly perhaps, not even faith—no, the greatest of these is *love.* Sure, Paul and Apollos do their part with their gifts, but the results depend on God. The Corinthians themselves, as a community, are

---

How do they resist the cult of personality and narcissism and hunger for power that can come from followers who idolize them? Paul says there's only one way—adopt the Logic of the Cross.

God's field and God's building. Notice the word "you" is plural ("y'all") and not singular—this is about a community, not just individual people.

Second, how are Paul and Apollos able to be grounded and humble, spiritually mature, working together instead of competing, understanding that one plants and another waters and neither is better or worse than the other? How do they resist the cult of personality and narcissism and hunger for power that can come from followers who idolize them? Paul says there's only one way—adopt the Logic of the Cross: "When I came to you, brothers and sisters, I did not come proclaiming the mystery of God to you in lofty words or wisdom. For I decided to know nothing among you except Jesus Christ, and him crucified" (1 Corinthians 2:1-2). (Refer to "The Christ Hymn" of Philippians 2:5-11, where Paul calls the community to "let the same mind be in you that was in Christ Jesus" [Philippians 2:5]).

To have "the mind of Christ" (1 Corinthians 2:16) is to practice choosing love and humility over and over again. Division and bickering seem to come easily, even though they cause stress, not peace. Unity takes intentional practice. Disagreement arises over what should be considered essential or nonessential, and I'm guessing you could name an example or two from your own community this moment. Healthy disagreement can lead to insight and growth. It can lead to a decision for those in disagreement to part ways with one another maturely and form new productive partnerships with others.

How can we possibly discern what's essential and what's not? Paul reminds us that we have the Holy Spirit to guide our communal discernment, should we be open to it. We can have the mind of Christ because here and now and always we have access to the Holy Spirit: "Y'all know that y'all are God's temple and that God's Spirit dwells among y'all, right?" (1 Corinthians 3:16, my translation). Truly spiritual people don't boast about how spiritual they are since the ego has moved aside to make room for the Spirit. As Paul says: "the Spirit searches everything, even the depths of God" (1 Corinthians 2:10). This same Spirit is the one that teaches human beings all we need to know about God and provides us access to direct encounters and experiences of God, many of which cannot be expressed fully by finite human language and categories of knowledge. It is by this Spirit "that we may understand the gifts bestowed on us by God" (1 Corinthians 2:12).

As we work toward discernment and unity, I recall Augustine of Hippo, who is credited with saying: "In essentials, unity; in non-essentials, liberty; in all things, love." The last clause is an excellent place to begin (and end): love. It calls to mind 1 Corinthians 13:13: "And now faith, hope, and love abide, these three; and the greatest of these is love." The Logic of the Cross is the Logic of Love; thus at every moment, in times of peace or in times of conflict, we can ask if we are regarding the other person or group with love.

Full of the Spirit or Just Hot Air? (1 Corinthians 3)

I find it encouraging that Paul simultaneously calls the Corinthians saints and spiritual babies who are so immature that he can only give them spiritual milk at the moment (I also like that here, as elsewhere, Paul depicts himself as a nursing mother):

> *And so, brothers and sisters, I could not speak to you as spiritual people, but rather as people of the flesh, as infants in Christ. I fed you with milk, not solid food, for you were not ready for solid food.*
>
> 1 Corinthians 3:1-2

There's certainly nothing wrong with starting out life as a baby, where everything is new and you are the center of the world. My granddaughter is five weeks old as I write this. For one month her parents have been pouring nonstop energy into her and, in return, she's rewarding all their hard work by sleeping, eating, and creating diaper-changing opportunities, just like she's supposed to. If she develops along a typical path, she will discover her power and her talents, and we will hear a fair amount of, "Hey, watch me! Watch me again!" She will eventually grow up, eat solid food, and learn that she is not the only show in town (and her grandparents will try not to insist that her show is still the best). She will learn how not just to be served but to serve others as well. She will mature and assume her place in God's order of things, helping to grow and build God's field, God's building.

Ironically, some of the key problems in the Corinthian church were caused by the self-designated "spiritual people" [*pneumatikoi*]. *Pneuma* is a Greek word that means spirit, breath, or wind, and these people were definitely full of hot air. Paul describes them as "puffed up" [*physiō*; 1 Corinthians 4:6]. Stop here and fill your cheeks up with air, and then say out loud forcefully, FOO-SEE-AH-OH. It's onomatopoeia, where the word sounds like the thing itself (like "buzz"). If there's one takeaway warning from 1 Corinthians, let it be this—do NOT be FOO-SEE-AH-OH. Isn't Greek fun?

According to Paul, the claims of the *pneumatikoi* are threefold: (1) they have knowledge (*gnōsis*, a word that comes up a lot in 1 Corinthians); (2) they are spiritual [*pneumatikoi*]; (3) as a result, they believe they have freedom to behave any way they want no matter how it affects others. They fancy themselves superior to others and accountable to no one. They are full of themselves, they boast, they are "puffed up," they cause factiousness, and they contribute to numerous moral problems and personal hurt in the church. As we will learn later, their motto is "all things are lawful for me."

Paul responds, "'All things are lawful for me,' but not all things are *beneficial*" (1 Corinthians 6:12, emphasis added).

They link their wisdom with the possession of the Spirit and they use it to act immorally and boast about it. Paul insists that those with true wisdom (read 1 Corinthians 2:10), those who understand the cross, are the mature Christians whose possession of the Spirit leads to cooperation and humility.

Reread 3:18-23 and pay attention to how the themes of wisdom versus foolishness and divisions (around Paul, Apollos, and so forth) versus cooperation in Christ come together and wrap up everything Paul's been getting at. Notice how he uses irony, paradox, and contrast. It's really quite brilliant and inspiring.

> *If you think that you are wise in this age, you should become fools so that you may become wise. For the wisdom of this world is foolishness with God....*
>
> *So let no one boast about human leaders. For all things are yours, whether Paul or Apollos or Cephas or the world or life or death or the present or the future—all belong to you, and you belong to Christ, and Christ belongs to God.*
>
> *1 Corinthians 3:18-23*

We can breathe into humility, aware of and grateful for our particular gifts, knowing our place in the family of things, confident in our unbroken, unbreakable connection to all that has ever been or will be, knowing that, finally, it all begins and ends with God, all depends on God. How freeing.

"And Furthermore": Paul's Leadership Style (1 Corinthians 4)

I remember my counselor Rachel helping me work through parenting a teenager. I would present the issue at hand and she would ask me how

I might respond. "Well, I would probably say" and then I'd launch into my proposed speech. Then Rachel would say: "Fewer words. They aren't listening after twenty seconds." In addition to keeping it brief, the trick was to avoid being "judgy Jaime" and, instead, convey the message using the skills of Nonviolent Communication (NVC), established by Marshall B. Rosenberg. On my best days, I would go home and do just that and while it may not compare to Paul's eloquent rhetoric in 1 Corinthians 3:18-23, I'd say it wasn't half bad and harmony and connection won the day. On my less effective days, not trusting that positive, inviting approach to be compelling enough, I'd go on to add some (very wordy) potential threats and ultimatums, just in case.

Reading 1 Corinthians 4 shows me that Paul himself had such days. There he moves from irony to outright sarcasm and trades transcendence for threat. The Corinthian Christians think they are "all that" and they boast about how blessed they are as evidenced by their charmed, superior lives that, clearly, they especially deserve. Paul replies, "Really. Wow. Interesting. If that's the standard we're using, if that's what wisdom really looks like, then I guess that makes us apostles fools." He puts them in their place by contrasting these arrogant fractious folks with him and Apollos.

> *I have applied all this to Apollos and myself for your benefit, brothers and sisters, so that you may learn through us the meaning of the saying, "Nothing beyond what is written," so that none of you will be puffed up in favor of one against another. For who sees anything different in you? What do you have that you did not receive?* And if you received it, why do you boast as if it were not a gift?
>
> *1 Corinthians 4:6-7, emphasis added*

Then comes the sarcasm. If you are able, read it aloud and emphasize the words I've emphasized. The "already" emphasizes that they truly believe they've "arrived," as we say. The *we* and *you* are to show the ironic contrast:

> Already *you have all you want!* Already *you have become rich! Quite apart from us you have become kings! Indeed, I wish that you had become kings, so that we might be kings with you! For I think that God has exhibited us apostles as last of all, as though sentenced to death, because we have become a spectacle to the world, to angels and to mortals.* We are *fools for the sake of Christ,* but you are *wise in Christ.* We are *weak,* but you are *strong.* You are *held in honor,* but we *in disrepute.*
>
> *1 Corinthians 4:8-10, emphasis added*

Now for the time-honored parent guilt: "I am not writing this to make you ashamed, but to admonish you as my beloved children. For though you might have ten thousand guardians in Christ, you do not have many fathers. Indeed, in Christ Jesus I became your father through the gospel" (vv. 14-15). Then comes the "I taught you better than this" move. In verses 16-17 Paul reminds the Corinthians that they have the example of Paul himself and that he has sent Timothy along to remind them of what they have learned and how that connects them to the wider Christian community beyond their hometown. Finally, the "don't make me come in there" threat: "What would you prefer? Am I to come to you with a stick, or with love in a spirit of gentleness?" (v. 21). Paul may just need a refresher course in NVC!

Joking aside, in all of his letters Paul demonstrates deep commitment and concern for those in the churches he establishes. He considers them family, referring to himself sometimes as a sibling, sometimes a father, sometimes a wet nurse who breastfeeds them, sometimes a mother (consult Galatians 4:19). All are very intimate, involved descriptors.

In addition to relating to his people as family, a second tactic Paul uses is pointing them to good examples of discipleship. Sometimes that entails following his lead, as in 1 Corinthians 11:1, "Become imitators of me just as I am an imitator of Christ" (my translation). Imitating Paul as he imitates Jesus certainly gives our lives meaningful shape and purpose, but it likely also leads to some amount of suffering, sacrifice, and interpersonal conflict.

Paul knew for certain that if we're going to stay the course with any perseverance, joy, or hope, we're going to have to do it **together.**

Standing up to the powers that be in the church and in the world on behalf of the "weak in the world," the "low and despised in the world," whom God has chosen in a very intentional specific way (1 Corinthians 1:27-28) may not win us approval from anyone but God; but what other approval is worth seeking anyway?

Paul knew for certain that if we're going to stay the course with any perseverance, joy, or hope, we're going to have to do it *together*. Some people have the impression that Paul was an autocrat, but the evidence proves quite the opposite. He cooperates and networks and depends upon an innumerable list of people. Notice that almost every Pauline letter is actually cowritten. For example, he cowrites 1 Corinthians with Sosthenes. Think of fellow workers he names just in 1 Corinthians alone (Timothy, Chloe, Apollos, Cephas) as he writes about the way one plants and another waters. If you really want to absorb this point, just read through Romans 16 where you will be astonished by the team effort on display.

Closing Thoughts

In this chapter, we have oriented ourselves to Corinth, the Corinthians, and Paul's correspondence with them. We have determined that the Logic of the Cross, which is the Logic of Love, is the overarching theme of the letter, the drumbeat that sounds throughout the letter and gives it coherence. We focused on the issue of divisions raised in these chapters along with Paul's proposed solutions. We also gave attention to the way Paul goes about pastoring them, his style, strategy, and some tactics. As we turn our attention to 1 Corinthians 5–7 in the next chapter, we will take everything we've learned in this chapter along with us, building upon that foundation and expanding our inquiry. The chapters ahead will touch upon an array of other joys and challenges that the community experienced. Let's discover what they have to teach us in light of our own context.

CHAPTER 2

Relationship Status: It's Complicated

In this chapter, I focus on three topics that arise from 1 Corinthians 5–7. First, sexual ethics. Second, Paul's gender equality, which I address in the midst of our discussion of sexual ethics. Third, eschatology and ethics. The last one seems heady, I know, but the fact is that you have some view of where things are headed. What difference, if at all, does it make for Christian ethics—and interpretation of Scripture—whether you think the world is ending in your lifetime or not?

Sexual Ethics: What We Do with Our Bodies, Others' Bodies, and What It Says about What We Believe

When it comes to sexual ethics, the Corinthians have too much and not enough. On the one hand, we have a man sleeping with his stepmom (5:1), men having sex with prostituted people (6:15-16), and men committing pederasty (6:9; adult males sexually preying on young males). On the other hand we have married people *refraining* from sex thinking it somehow makes them extra holy to deny such pleasure. Let's just say that these chapters are anything but dull. Stop having sex. Have more sex. Try not to start having sex. Yes, all three of these are advice that Paul gives different people in 1 Corinthians 5–7, and the variations in his advice should signal to us right away that Paul is not writing a timeless treatise on sex (or sexual orientation or gender for that matter). He is, in turn, taking up very specific situations, and there is no one-size-fits-all answer at that level. If one is asking for the principle at work in the varied individual prescriptions (that is, the spirit of the law rather than the letter of the law), then the ethical instruction is actually the same: love God and love your neighbor, who is created in the image of God and "for whom Christ died" (1 Corinthians 8:11).

In this section, we discuss two of the three pieces of advice Paul gives to the Corinthians: "Stop having sex," and "Have more sex." Then, in the next section, we'll take up the third line of counsel Paul gives the Corinthians, and we'll tie it in to his eschatology.

Destructive Sex

Let's start with the folks in Corinth who imagine life as nothing but one long Florida spring break or Las Vegas trip. In fact, so notorious was the city of Corinth in general for its Vegas-like features that there was a Greek verb "to act like a Corinthian" that referred to engaging in sexual immorality. The slogan of these specific Corinthian Christians in our text is "All things are lawful for me" (6:12). Jesus has come, history has wrapped up, let's live like there's no tomorrow.

Now, it's true that Paul taught that Christians should live like there's no tomorrow, as we will discover later, but he means something different by it (spoiler alert—he wants Christians to be mindfully present to the moment in a way that brings wholeness to the world). It's also true that Paul taught the Gentile Christians that they did not have to get circumcised or follow the Jewish law with respect to food. What Paul *said* and what the immature Corinthians *heard* sounds a lot like what happens when parents speak to children: "You can use the car. Here are the keys." You meant they could use it to go to their friend's house and come back home, not go joyriding all over town. Paul makes a statement, and they take it to the extreme.

Sex and Shared Communal Values (1 Corinthians 5)

Chapter 5 finds a man sleeping with his stepmom, which Paul finds problematic. Equally problematic in Paul's estimation is the fact that no one questions the man about how this might violate the shared values of the church at Corinth. Paul tells the Corinthians to intervene and, if the man chooses to disregard the intervention, to put him out of the community. A few words are in order here. I experience a tension when reading about this situation. On the one hand, I think it's important for a community to have both a generally agreed upon set of ethical values and expectations to which members can aspire and a way to lovingly, if firmly, intervene when someone is behaving unethically and destructively. Thus, I think it's essential for Christian communities not to sweep destructive behavior under the rug.

On the other hand, such conversations raise concerns about practices of shaming and humiliating people in the name of God or sanctimonious self-righteousness. Students tell me about certain traditions that have "mourning benches" or "sinner's benches" up in the front or pastors who "call individuals out for their sins" publicly when the community is gathered. That is nothing but an abuse of power combined with inexcusable ignorance. In addition, I worry about the list of offenses that land one on the "shaming bench" as well as who gets to decide that. So there are two sides to the issue. Opportunities for abuse abound; yet, communities must have some discernible shared values to cohere as a community.

In this instance, the Corinthians swing wildly from taking a "live and let live," "you do *you*, bro" to the opposite extreme of casting the man out into eternal banishment after reading Paul's letter here. We surmise this from 2 Corinthians 2:5-11, where we read about Paul having to encourage the

Corinthians to accept this man back into the community, saying, in effect, "Yes, I asked you to confront this man about his behavior so he could do some soul-searching and decide whether he does, in fact, share the values of the community and wants to continue being part of it." Repentance. Followed by forgiveness and reconciliation. That's the Christian way. But the Corinthians tend toward extremes. Reading it, it's easy to shake my head and ask, "Honestly, what's wrong with these people?" But then I think about all the ways I (and some churches) act just like they do! From one extreme to the other, missing the point on both ends.

How much accountability is there in churches for our behavior, and how does this work in a healthy (not twisted, traumatic) way? Some churches are cult-like and too in-your-business; others, maybe not enough. How does your church deal with such issues?

Using People as Objects (1 Corinthians 6)

The man in chapter 5 may have been beyond the pale for Paul, but presumably the sex was consensual. In chapter 6, however, we arrive at the nadir of human sexuality, where people use others as mere objects for self-gratification. For anyone inclined to bury their head in the sand, the Me Too movement, not to mention the scandals in the church across denominations, has courageously emboldened us to bring all of our best intentions, resources, strategies, and tactics to the table to create spaces of honesty, action, and even redemption.

If we are tempted to think this sort of behavior—even the most grotesque—is a thing of the past, we are devastatingly wrong. And, while it's difficult to talk about, we can't afford to ignore it. For instance, child pornography is a staggeringly lucrative industry.

In the Gentile (non-Jewish) Roman world of the first century (and we could talk about today), men were entitled to sex with prostitutes of all genders as well as their wives, concubines, and slaves of any gender.

Some Corinthians insist on this slogan: "All things are lawful for me." Paul takes their point but tempers it: "but not all things are beneficial."

And, pederasty was accepted. Into this context, Paul the Jew, Roman citizen, and apostle to the Gentiles speaks a new and different word about sexual ethics. The kinds of sexual relationships Paul opposes here have in common the lack of respect for the fact that the sexual partner is a person, created by God in the image of God, not just another item for consumption.

Instead, some Corinthians insist on this slogan: "All things are lawful for me." Paul takes their point but tempers it: "but not all things are beneficial." Again, they insist, "All things are lawful for me." Paul does not overtly rebuke this statement but counters in an indirect way: "but I will not be dominated by anything" (6:12). "Food is meant for the stomach and the stomach for food" (6:13), they say as they justify their excessive consumption as a God-given right. Where they insist on their rights in an absolute sense, Paul constantly sets their so-called "rights" into a larger perspective of how they can use those rights to build others up.

My friend Roy tells a story from when his son, Noah, was in high school: "One of his favorite bands came to our city for a concert. The concert was downtown late at night in a sprawling metroplex, and Noah had only been driving a few months. He asked rather passionately, 'Can I go?'" To this, Roy responded, "Of course. You can *do* whatever you want. Anything that you want to do, you can, of course, do. Of course, you might get killed, or get arrested, or hurt people, or regret it later. On the other hand, you might have a great time and nothing bad will happen. But, yes, you can *do* whatever you want. The question isn't 'Can I?' The real question is: 'Should I?'... and that is a very different question." Noah did go and had a wonderful time. But the tagline, "Of course, you can *do* anything you want…" has stuck around in this family ever since.

Using the bodies of others, and especially those who have no choice, is incommensurate with the Logic of Love. Not only does it distort the face of God in the other, but in the end it does the same to ourselves. The act of sex should be one in which those participating are treated as persons made in the image of God, nothing less. In every particular example related to sex (but not only sex) that Paul addresses, these are the recurring themes: mutuality, respect for the other person as made in the image of God, and an insistence that what we do with our bodies is inherently tied to the health of our souls.

Some people may read 1 Corinthians 6 and condemn two groups of modern people, prostituted people and members of the LGBTQIA+ community, as sexual deviants who don't belong in the Christian community. But both moves are problematic on numerous counts. While the subject is larger than I can fully treat here, a few brief words are in order.[1] First, Paul lived in the first century with notions of biology and gender that do not cohere with modern knowledge (feel free to read the works of the most famous doctor of that period, Galen, and be thankful he isn't practicing his medicine on you, especially if you are a female). Second, given the power relations of ancient society, the issue at hand is how those with power and status use or abuse it with respect to other people's bodies. Then as now, human trafficking was lucrative, and those with money used the bodies of those who had no power and status.

Third, Paul is a Jew in the first century operating within a particular sexual ethic. We may or may not agree with every detail of Paul's view of sexual activity, but it's important to highlight the main point: Christians should behave as Christ would. Paul has the Corinthians take seriously the notion of Christ living in them, so that, with every move they make with their bodies, they are to ask: Is this what Christ would do? Is this how Jesus would interact with this person? Am I treating this person as the precious treasure of God that they are or as an object for my use and goals? That, I would maintain, is a timeless Christian truth, even though we now know way more about biology, gender, and science than Paul did.

Edifying Sex (1 Corinthians 7:1-9)

Can't Touch This?

As we have noted above, Paul doesn't tell the folks in chapters 5 and 6 to stop having sex because sex is bad. In fact, chapter 7 opens with Paul calling another set of Corinthians to have more sex! We are now familiar with "Corinthian slogans"—pronouncements that some Corinthians proclaim but Paul counters. In this case, we learn of married people avoiding sex, thinking themselves to be holier by denying the body: "It is well for a man not to touch a woman" (7:1). They have heard Paul say in person that he prefers that people do *not* get married if at all possible, let alone have children (we'll discuss why in the following section). This makes it sound like marriage and sex are beneath Christians, so some of these ascetic Corinthian couples have stopped having sex. But that's not Paul's intention.

Hunk of Burning Love? Go for It.

It's important to note that throughout his writings Paul insists on embodiment as a good, godly reality (after all, God chose to create us as embodied and called that creation "good"), so much so that Paul insists that we will have bodies in the resurrection. So here, Paul contests the Corinthians' asceticism by calling them to tend to one another's sexual needs in a mutual way. In the case of these married people, he assumes that sexual desire and passion are part of what brought them together so that to repress those desires is more likely to lead to destructive sexual immorality than super-holiness. So, he advises them to ditch the contrived restraint and enjoy God's good creation! Similarly, in 7:8-9, Paul tells those who aren't married, including widows, to get married if their sexual desire calls for it.

I want to highlight the language of mutuality in Paul's counsel. Paul's countercultural sexual ethics where every body is to be treated with dignity and respect didn't apply just to prostitutes and other socially powerless people. It also applied between married people regardless of gender. What Paul says about a husband, he says equally about a wife. No one in antiquity is writing home about the idea of a husband having authority over his wife's body or a wife giving her husband conjugal rights (not the most romantic depiction of marital romance), but the fact that Paul explicitly states that *the wife has authority over her husband's body* and that he owes *her* conjugal rights is astounding. Naming and validating female sexual desire, and mentioning *first* that the husband should consider the wife's sexual needs, is most certainly ancient headline news (and maybe even news in modern times)! Regulating female sexuality was the order of the day. In each case that Paul addresses, what's good for the goose is good for the gander. Read line by line through verse 16 and you will find he doesn't just address one gender and assume the other will apply it; rather, he addresses each back and forth. Given the high cost of papyrus and ink back then, repeating that for each gender is noteworthy.

My, Look at the Time! Ethics and Eschatology

As we've discussed, all of Paul's advice to the Corinthians is shaped by the ethic of "love God and love neighbor." Some of Paul's advice—both relationship advice and advice about other life circumstances—is also shaped by his eschatology, his view of the end of the world. In particular, Paul believed that the world as we know it would soon be forever changed by Jesus coming back and completely transforming all of heaven and earth. Paul turned out to be wrong on this, which caused the early Christians to have to decide how to set up life in a world that may not, in fact, be ending soon. This "challenge" is referred to as the Delay of the Parousia (the Greek word *parousia* means "arrival," and it is used in this sense in reference to what is sometimes called "the Second Coming" by some modern Christians, though that phrase never appears in Scripture), and we find authors after Paul responding to it (consult Ephesians, Colossians, and 1–2 Timothy, for example). But Paul didn't know he'd be wrong, and he gives advice in light of his convictions.

Going to the Chapel of Love? Try Not To (1 Corinthians 7:8-16, 25-40)

Repeatedly in 1 Corinthians 7, Paul actually expresses a desire that people avoid getting married if they can reasonably help it. This sentiment first shows up in 7:8-9, where Paul tells any who aren't married, including widows, that "it is well for them to remain unmarried as I am," although he counsels that any who are "aflame with passion" should go ahead and marry, as we've already discussed. It shows up again in 7:25-40, where Paul addresses some of the responsibilities that come along with having a family. But Paul doesn't *just* tell people not to get married if they can help it. There's also a larger principle at work here: *whatever* their relationship status, people should remain as they are, married or unmarried. Notice *why* it is that Paul gives this advice:

> *I think that, in view of the impending crisis, it is well for you to remain as you are. Are you bound to a wife? Do not seek to be free. Are you free from a wife? Do not seek a wife. But if you marry, you do not sin, and if a virgin marries, she does not sin. Yet those who marry will experience distress in this life, and I would spare you that.*
>
> *1 Corinthians 7:26-28*

"In view of the impending crisis" is Paul's way of referring to Jesus's return. So while there's nothing wrong with getting married and having children (clearly, since Paul tells married people to stay married), a mortgage, and a 401(k), it doesn't make sense if it's all ending soon.

Ultimately, in 1 Corinthians 7, Paul wants people—across genders—not to worry about their marital status but to devote themselves fully to serving the gospel and evangelizing, just as he does (we'll find that in 1 Corinthians 9:19-23). Importantly, he does not condemn those who are married or who have a strong desire or need to partner because of sexual desire (though, one potential problem with Paul's view is that he almost reduces marriage to sex). And he *certainly* believes it's better to marry than run around doing the kinds of things we found in chapters 5 and 6, making choices that are potentially destructive to other people. But he believes spreading the gospel is a top priority that is easier to do without family concerns. And again, notice that Paul expects the same thing from both males and females:

> *I mean, brothers and sisters, the appointed time has grown short. . . . For the present form of this world is passing away.*
>
> *I want you to be free from anxieties. The unmarried man is anxious about the affairs of the Lord, how to please the Lord; but the married man is anxious about the affairs of the world, how to please his wife, and his interests are divided. And the unmarried woman and the virgin are anxious about the affairs of the Lord, so that they may be holy in body and spirit; but the married woman is anxious about the affairs of the world, how to please her husband. I say this for your own benefit, not to put any restraint upon you, but to promote good order and unhindered devotion to the Lord.*
>
> *1 Corinthians 7:29-35*

Now if Paul doesn't want people to get married because it takes time and energy, he certainly doesn't promote having children. It's noteworthy that both Jesus and Paul, two Jewish men from a culture that expects men to get married and have children (Rome, which occupied the known world of our New Testament authors, had very particular ideas about "family values" and made laws that rewarded marrying and having children), are never explicitly depicted as having a wife or children. Neither do they expect women to be valued on the basis of having children. Paul argues quite the opposite—he wants women to do exactly what he calls the men to do, with no difference at all. All of this is countercultural to the max.

Just as Paul's preaching, which we have inherited, speaks into our own lives, it has been speaking into lives for numerous generations before us. Have you ever read the early Christian work called *The Acts of Paul and Thecla*? If you haven't, you must. It's tightly connected to 1 Corinthians 7. Thecla, who is engaged to be married to a guy named Thamyris, hears Paul preach the very content that we find here, and she is called into ministry to serve the gospel. She dresses like a man (a countercultural move due to her sexist culture), and off she goes, choosing to remain unmarried for the sake of ministry. Her fiancé and her mom are both angry, and they try to get her and Paul killed. Her mother tells the town officials they should burn her daughter at the stake as an example to other young women who might get uppity ideas about not getting married and having children and trotting off to preach about this gospel stuff. But Thecla survives, has many impressive experiences, and a whole religious trajectory builds up around her in Egypt.

Thecla is one example of a woman who took Paul seriously, followed the call, and invoked the wrath of her family and society by doing so. Nevertheless, she persisted, and God blessed her vocation. She is joined by the likes of St. Perpetua and St. Felicitas. Again, if those names are new to you, you will want to read their extremely poignant stories sooner rather than later. Each of them hears the call to serve God in unorthodox ways. Each of them recognizes the truth in Paul's preaching that people are called according to gifts, not gender.

Before we turn from Paul's sexual ethics, I want to point out that, whether Paul is addressing sexual libertines or sexual ascetics or anyone in between, he concedes that different people are called differently sexually and in interpersonal relationships. What I want you to grasp is this: on the one hand, there's no right answer to whether a person should or shouldn't get married and whether they should or shouldn't have sex—that is different for different people. On the other hand, there is most *certainly* one right answer: our choices should reflect gospel-living, which means loving, mutual relationships, sexual or otherwise, that build each other up and recognize the image of God in the other. The litmus test in 1 Corinthians is love, whether for you that means getting married or not, having sex or not. Let *love* (not purity, not ego, not power) guide your choice.

The Downside of Paul's Advice to "Remain as You Are"

Above, we saw the ways that Paul's advice to "remain as you are" freed people to do ministry in a wider context. People like Thecla, freed from the cultural demand to find her worth in marriage and procreation, could follow their call. Other people, called to marriage and the joys and demands of family, could likewise embrace their call. For all of these groups, "remain as you are" was "good news," a word of validation and liberation. But what about those enslaved, those for whom the status quo (to stay as they are) is bad news?

Let's review. Paul's relationship advice is influenced by each of the following considerations:

1. checking one's choices against the standards of the community to which one has committed and whose values one claims to share;
2. using power and privilege ethically, not using people as objects;
3. having a relationship with one's partner in which each person's needs and desires are discussed and honored;
4. believing that the end of the world is near.

The first three, with some conversation, most likely cohere well with how modern Christians think through some ethical issues. The last one, however, does not cohere as readily with our understanding of reality (after all, we are still here long after Paul imagined we would be) and, in fact, is unfortunately tied to some seriously problematic—even morally reprehensible—ethical stances. This can be seen, for example, with the issue of slavery, which also appears in chapter 7.

Paul addresses Christians in Corinth who are slaves, and thus are at the bottom of the social hierarchy:

> *Were you a slave when called? Do not be concerned about it. Even if you can gain your freedom, make use of your present condition now more than ever. For whoever was called in the Lord as a slave is a freed person belonging to the Lord, just as whoever was free when called is a slave of Christ.*
>
> 1 Corinthians 7:21-22

What goes through your mind when you read this? Are you shocked that Paul seems to treat slavery so cavalierly? Maybe you are wondering some of the following questions: Is Paul telling slaves to stay in slavery even if they have a chance to get out? Does Paul promote slavery? If he doesn't believe slavery is God's will, why doesn't he just say it: "Humans should not own other humans"?

To get ahold of the issue, let's sort through what Paul says here and elsewhere about slavery. First, notice Paul's typical use of irony and paradox, which emphasize that God's values are different from the world's. Those Corinthians who are mere slaves in the world's social hierarchy are free spiritually; those Corinthians who are free (like Paul) are slaves to Christ, which, ironically, is the freest position imaginable from Paul's perspective, as he says in Galatians 5:1: "For freedom Christ has set us free." He means spiritually free. Recall Viktor Frankl, Holocaust survivor and author of *Man's Search for Meaning*. Dr. Frankl was imprisoned by the Nazis in World War II because he was a Jew. His wife, parents, and brother were all killed in concentration camps during the Holocaust. Having lost his family and his material possessions, with nothing but his malnourished, beaten, naked body, Frankl was able to declare: "Everything can be taken from a man but one thing: the last of the human freedoms—to choose one's attitude in any given set of circumstances, to choose one's own way."[2] In a similar manner, we find Paul redefining slavery and freedom, power and weakness.

Second, in his letter to Philemon, Paul asks Philemon to welcome back the (runaway?) slave Onesimus not just as a slave but as a Christian sibling. Paul may even be asking Philemon to free Onesimus. And in his profoundly important, earth-shaking baptismal pronouncement in Galatians 3:28, Paul declares: "There is no longer Jew or Greek, there is no longer slave or free, there is no longer male and female; for all of you are one in Christ Jesus." One can look at Paul's own enacted ministry and observe that he expected Christians *already* to live on earth as it is in heaven, where such binaries and hierarchies do not exist. For instance, in Galatians 2, Paul confronts Peter for making a distinction between Jews and Gentiles. Throughout his ministry, we find women and men fulfilling the same roles—minister, apostle, leaders of house churches, coworkers and fellow prisoners with Paul—for the sake of the gospel. And then there's Onesimus. Thus, by reading Paul's undisputed letters (unlike the later letters written in his name, Ephesians and Colossians), we have every reason to believe that Paul himself considered slavery part of the "foolishness of this world," part of the "present form of this world that is passing away."

But does Paul anywhere call for the empire-wide immediate abolition of slavery? No, nowhere, unfortunately. This reality, along with the Household Codes of Ephesians, Colossians, and 1 Peter, gave proslavery American Christians cheap, easy proof texts to insist that owning slaves was ordained by God. We Christians in 2021 know, however, that enslavement of Africans in America is a shameful, morally reprehensible part of our history whose evil still infects our shared lives. What, then, do we do with texts such as 1 Corinthians 7:21-22 so that we avoid that same danger of using our Scriptures to oppress others? Well, we must put on our thinking caps and do the hard work of reading the texts in light of their ancient

Paul thought the world was ending any minute, so he wanted all hands on deck to spread the gospel in every way possible.

literary and historical contexts before we determine how to apply Scripture ethically to our lives.

Paul's comments on whether or not a slave should seek freedom are part of the same larger literary unit that spans most of chapter 7. We've noted that elsewhere in this chapter (7:8, 26) Paul advises people to stay the course in their current relationship status for the sake of the gospel. Here, Paul considers other types of life situations in which people find themselves at the moment, and, no matter the circumstance, he's got one solution: "Let each of you remain in the condition in which you were called" (7:20). Thus, Paul is not here (or anywhere) answering the question, "Is slavery ethical?" He's addressing the subject of whether anyone should seek to change their current social situation, and slavery is one such circumstance he mentions.

And, again, at that point in time, Paul thought the world was ending any minute, so he wanted all hands on deck to spread the gospel in every way possible. Paul wasn't proslavery, just as he didn't hate marriage or kids. That is, in each case he gave advice to remain in one's present condition only because he thought Jesus was coming back right away. That is, his ethics were influenced by his eschatology, which is true for all of us. If you have a 401(k) or an education fund for your grandchildren or put the longer lasting roof on your house, you have a different eschatology than Paul. You expect you and your descendants to have to manage life on this planet, in this creation, for some time to come.

We wonder what he would have advised if he had imagined us still being here thousands of years later. Would he have married that "believing wife" he mentions in chapter 9? We can't know, and we don't need to because we have the Holy Spirit to help us think through how Christians are to live in the world of 2021, which has some things in common with the first-century church and world, but not all.

That brings me to another important aspect of all this. Not only do we not know what Paul might say in every circumstance, Paul did not know—or pretend to know—what Jesus might teach in every situation. In fact, in 7:10, 7:12, 7:25, and 7:40, Paul freely concedes that at some points he has the teachings of Jesus to rely on and at other points, he does not. For example, in 7:10 Paul refers to a teaching about divorce that comes from Jesus (although most churches in 2021 do not practice this "rule" about divorce from the first century, given our different context). But at 7:12 (and 7:25) we have the opposite example where Paul patently does not have a word from Jesus and clarifies that it's his opinion.

I respect Paul's honesty about the fact that we don't have ready, easy answers but have to work through important ethical considerations using a mixture of Scripture, tradition, reason, and experience, aided by the Holy Spirit: "And I think that I too have the Spirit of God" (7:40). Paul is making it up as he goes based on what he thinks he knows, on Jesus, and on the Spirit. Not a bad start for anyone. And, as we seek to do the same, perhaps we can apply the principle of Paul's message—going all out for the gospel—and even reach a completely different conclusion regarding slavery. That is, perhaps we can pour ourselves into the necessary work of ushering in "on earth as it is in heaven" to work to eradicate all forms of slavery, including sexual slavery, in our world today. Perhaps in so doing we are being faithful to the underlying principle of Paul's teaching.

Closing Thoughts 

In this chapter, we learned that 1 Corinthians 5–7 is filled with guidance about Christian sexual (and other sorts of) relationships. We also learned that Paul's ethical advice was shaped by his belief that the world was ending very soon.

Some "takeaways" we might consider from this chapter are as follows:

1. First Corinthians 5–7 teaches us respect for other people's bodies.
2. First Corinthians 5–7 teaches us how to serve God even if it goes against the "traditional family values" of a particular empire or culture.
3. The story of St. Thecla (and St. Perpetua and St. Felicitas) shows that Paul's preaching led to certain women choosing to opt out of partnering and childbearing. This led to a backlash that we see in 1 Timothy where women are instructed to shut up, get married, be submissive, and have babies—indeed, the author of 1 Timothy avers that women will, in fact, be "*saved* through childbearing" (2:15, emphasis added). Obviously, 1 Corinthians 7 and 1 Timothy 2 represent very different views of women's vocations.
4. Christians need to align their ethics with their eschatology. We cannot *both* store up our 401(k) *and* simultaneously act like we think that the world is ending and Jesus is coming back tomorrow. *Either* you think we're here for a while—so you should care about systems of justice *on earth*, here and *now* and use your resources to care for "the least of these"—*or* you think the world is ending tomorrow so, like Paul, you are using all your resources "becoming all things to all people that you might save some." One way or the other, be honest about your eschatology and then make choices consistent with it.
5. Watching Paul in these chapters invites Christians to be creative, to be intellectually agile, and to be like the scribe/Pharisee that is Paul, who, like Matthew, imaginatively combines what is old and what is new in an effort to share the gospel here and now, no matter what century the "here and now" involves! With Jesus as his starting point, Paul extrapolates into new territory and boldly acknowledges that he is doing so! May we be as creative, daring, transparent, and faithful in our own context.

CHAPTER 3

FREEDOM: FROM WHAT, FOR WHAT?

As seasoned readers of 1 Corinthians, we are not surprised by the *peri de* ("now concerning") at 8:1—it just indicates we are turning to another specific challenge this community is having. Neither are we surprised to come across more "Corinthian slogans" marked off in your modern translation by quotation marks in 8:1, 8:4, and 10:23. So what is the ancient problem Paul's addressing now, and how might it speak to our modern context?

At first when I explain the ancient problem, which is a question about whether or not Christians should eat meat sacrificed to idols, you might be tempted to skip over it or skim quickly because it sounds boring or irrelevant to our pressing concerns. But that would be a big mistake because 1 Corinthians 8–10 gets at the meat (pardon the pun) of the Logic of the Cross and what it means to be an ethical Christian. If you just had chapter 1 and chapters 8–10, you'd probably have enough to go on to understand Paul's Logic of the Cross (though of course we are all the richer for the whole record of the Corinthian correspondence). In this chapter, I will summarize the main issues and the information needed to grasp the ancient situation. Then I will suggest ways the past might speak into our present.

Background Information

First, it's important to know that in the first-century Roman Empire, just like in many places today, people with money eat meat and poor people eat grains.

Second, "religion" in ancient Rome consisted of two main prongs for worship and devotion. The first prong was the pantheon: worship of all those gods and goddesses you learned about in your high school English class. Every city had numerous temples to various gods and goddess. If you visit the ancient site of Corinth today, you'll be greeted by a huge Temple of Apollo. You will also see artifacts from the Temple of Asclepius, the ancient god of healing (more about this when we discuss 1 Corinthians 12). The second prong was expected participation in the Imperial Cult, worshipping the genius of the emperor. These two prongs constituted religion in antiquity, and it was everyone's patriotic duty to participate in this civic religion. If you want to get the feeling of it, think about how angry and emotional and hateful some Americans get when a person refuses to say the pledge of allegiance to the American flag or when a pastor tries to remove an American flag from an American sanctuary. That's how Romans felt about Jews and Christians who refused to worship false gods, including the emperor. As strange and ironic as it may sound to us, pagan (defined as non-Jewish or Christian) folks considered Christians to be atheists since Christians did not pay homage to civic religion—worshipping the gods of Rome. For Romans, before going to war, it was important to pray to the gods of war, just as it was important to pray to the gods who looked after the city or the crops. When Christians opted out of this civic religion, they were seen as subversive, unpatriotic atheists. Christians then, and now (on our best days), offer their devotion to God alone, no matter what country they reside in. Where Christians can be true to Jesus and adhere to the rules of a current government, that's fine. But when the two conflict, Christians ought to choose the way of Jesus.

On civic holidays associated with these various cults, animals would be sacrificed in honor of the gods and passed out to the people as part of the festivities. Kind of like a giant Fourth of July parade where they are passing out meat instead of candy from a float. Thus, the only time poor people would eat meat would be in this context in which the meat was "idol meat," from a Christian perspective, since Jews and Christians considered devotion to and worship of the emperor and pagan gods and goddesses to be idolatry. The tight association between meat and idolatry would not have been so strong for the wealthier Christians who were already used to eating meat in their regular lives (we will see again the challenges raised by having wealthier and poorer Christians in the same church in chapter 11, where Paul discusses the Lord's Supper). Now, before the Gentile Corinthians became Christians, there was no issue because they were all happily (and maybe even mindlessly) participating in the civic religion. But once they became Christians, these gods and the emperor now became "idols" *not* to be worshipped. This raised the question of whether eating the meat that had been slaughtered in the name of one or another god was participating in idolatry or not. In our Corinthians case, two specific issues are raised.

First, the educated ("knowledgeable" in Paul's words), wealthier Christians came to understand that these gods and the emperor are not really divine and don't have any power compared to the God of Jesus. For all practical purposes, they are not "real." We will call these Corinthians "the strong." On the other hand, there are other Christians who don't or can't grasp this fact, who are what we might call "superstitious" (Paul calls them those with a "weak conscience"), who carry some residual belief that there's something real (and spooky) about these pagan gods such that they think it's wrong to partake of the meat. So, one issue Paul addresses is how the strong Christians are supposed to act in light of the fact that the weak Christians are freaked out (unnecessarily, but freaked out all the same) by the idol meat. We will walk through his interesting argument that at first may seem complicated and certainly raises some questions for further discussion but which finally boils down to this: *when in doubt, adopt the Logic of the Cross.* If the idol meat is freaking out your superstitious brothers and sisters, then don't eat it in front of them, even though technically you have every right to. Paul gives a crucial lesson on the proper use of our authority and rights [*exousia*], as we will see.

The second issue has to do with when the strong, educated Christians are having their power lunches with their strong, educated non-Christian friends—should they eat idol meat in that situation? The short answer to that one is this: it depends on the situation. Paul is a strong proponent of situational ethics because he knows life is complex and a simplistic, one-size-fits-all rule is ineffective at best. The bedrock ethical principle for Christians is to *assess the details of the given situation from all angles and then adopt the Logic of the Cross.* It's sort of like the advice from Augustine: "Love, and do what thou wilt."[1] With Christ dwelling within us and the Holy Spirit guiding us, we don't need a laminated set of rules—we will do the Christlike thing that shows love for God and neighbor, even if it means not insisting on our way when it comes to something that is neither here nor there, which is called an *adiaphoron.* As we move into the details, we will see that there are certainly hills to die on (which Paul does) but not as many as we like to think or invent.

A Detailed Look at the Corinthian Situation (1 Corinthians 8)

The initial sentences (8:1-3) require some unpacking as we watch Paul unfold a deep, convicting point about what Christian knowledge, love, and community are all about. Paul makes a couple of moves worth noticing here. First, he acknowledges that the strong Christians have knowledge [*gnōsis*]; he never denies that. But he distinguishes between "knowledge"

Yes, we know stuff; but more importantly, we are **known.**

and "necessary knowledge." As he did earlier with power and wisdom in chapters 1–4, here he refines and redefines what "counts" from God's perspective, which is a view from the cross. There are two features I want to highlight about Paul's instruction in 1 Corinthians 8.

First, the most important point about knowledge and knowing is this: We are *known* (passive verb) by God. God knows us. God's knowledge is the gold standard, and we rest in the fact that we are known by God. When God loves and knows, edification, building up [*oikodomeō*] happens. God's knowledge and love lead to wholeness and salvation and integration and reconciliation with ourselves and others. God doesn't use God's knowledge to feed God's ego, to become puffed up. Unlike the queen in Snow White, God doesn't self-obsess, needing the mirror, mirror on the wall to say that God is fairest of them all. Yes, we know stuff; but more importantly, we are *known*. In case we miss it here, Paul will sound this theme again in 1 Corinthians 13:2, 8, and especially eloquently in 13:12: "Now we see in a mirror, dimly, but then we will see face to face. Now I know only in part; then I will know fully, even as I have been fully known." Mirror, mirror on the wall, who's the fairest of them all? The one who reflects God's fully revealed love.

Second, notice as we go that Paul always sides with the strong in principle but the weak in practice. He is one of the "strong"—he has knowledge, authority, and the rest of it, which is why he uses the word "we" and not "y'all"—"*we* know." He never asks them to play dumb or don a false modesty about their knowledge and power. He only asks them to train it toward service to others for God's sake.

Paul and the strong agree on God's sovereignty—God is not simply a member of the Greco-Roman pantheon. Thus, in 8:4 Paul says, "Hence, as to the eating of food offered to idols, *we* know that 'no idol in the world really exists,' and that 'there is no God but one'" (emphasis added). (The latter quotation alludes to the Shema from Deuteronomy 6:4, which Jesus recites in Mark 12:29. As Jews, Paul and Jesus would have recited the Shema regularly.) To paraphrase, the strong Corinthians, the ones Paul is addressing here, are saying, "We can eat this meat because *we* know Apollo isn't a real god—those 'gods' are just statues, lumps of wood. Thus, it would be stupid to deprive ourselves of this 'idol' meat because we all know that God is God and that's just a statue so what's the problem?" And Paul agrees, in principle.

The problem for Paul arises in 1 Corinthians 8:7. In effect he says, "Fine, you have knowledge. But not everyone does. Some people simply cannot dissociate eating that meat from participating in idol worship. So when they are in a situation where Christians are eating that meat, they are scandalized. Paul's actual words are "and their conscience, being weak, is defiled."

One can imagine the strong countering Paul again, saying, "Look, food is just food; it's not magical or angelic or demonic. It's just food. So who cares if we eat this steak or not? It's just steak."

For his part, Paul entirely grants their premise that the steak is just steak and it's neither here nor there; what he takes issue with is the fact that the strong insist on eating it even when they know that it is downright scandalous for the weaker-minded. If, indeed, the steak is "no big deal," then why, oh why must you *make* it a big deal by insisting on eating it in front of those who are hurt by your doing so? Perhaps you are doing it to throw your weight around, to use your freedom and authority to practically taunt others? In short, perhaps you are doing it to feed your own ego, to become puffed up.

Paul makes three strong points. First, he warns, "But take care that this liberty [*exousia*] of yours does not somehow become a stumbling block to the weak" (1 Corinthians 8:9). It's not about whether or not you have knowledge or liberty (you do); it's only about how you choose to use it. You always have a choice. Be careful not to become enslaved by your liberty.

Second, he tells them that how they treat others, especially the "weak," is registered as how they treat Christ. This line has always struck me with its shocking bluntness: "So by your knowledge those weak believers *for whom Christ died* are destroyed" (1 Corinthians 8:11, emphasis added). The weak ones mattered enough for Christ to die for but don't matter enough to y'all to forgo a steak for one meal? And if that were not clear enough, Paul says, "But when you thus sin against members of your family, and wound their conscience when it is weak, you sin against Christ" (1 Corinthians 8:12). These people are not some random "others." These people are your family, and if that's not compelling enough for you (maybe you don't like your family), then think about dissing them as dissing the very Christ you claim to follow! Dang! You might say, "Well, *that* escalated quickly." Or, "I don't think we're talking merely about steak anymore." Exactly. That's what Paul is saying. Pick an issue, fill in the blank, it doesn't matter. What behaviors on our part are compassionate and build up others, even if those people aren't as far along as we are on the spiritual path? Conversely, what behaviors on our part hinder others on their spiritual path? Do we need to "show off" our advanced wisdom and spirituality and trip others as we run onto the "spiritual winner's platform"?

Third, Paul clinches the argument by modeling the loving behavior that he's calling the strong to: "Therefore, if food is a cause of their falling [*skandalizō* in Greek], I will never eat meat, so that I may not cause one of them to fall" (1 Corinthians 8:13). Let's help each other up, not make each other fall.

Skipping over to chapter 10, Paul expressly gets back to the idol-meat controversy and at 10:23 we hear a familiar refrain (remember 1 Corinthians 6?) as he quotes the strong in Corinth: "All things are lawful [for us]" and responds with his signature "but not all things are beneficial." Again, they say, "All things are lawful," and he says, sure, "but not all things

How *one uses one's freedom to eat or not eat is everything.*

build up" [*oikodomeō*]; note the parallel to the opening of this session at 8:1. Then he gives yet another summary of the Logic of the Cross first presented in 1:18. "Do not seek your own advantage, but that of the other" (10:24). In this particular instance in chapter 10, he is addressing the issue of what a Christian should do if eating with a *non*-Christian and idol meat is on the menu. I'll let you read the details, but the short version is, *read the situation and decide what best serves the gospel.* If no one mentions the fact that the meat comes from the pagan ritual, eat up without comment. If the other person makes a point of mentioning it to see what you will do because their conscience is troubled, then refrain. The meat itself is an *adiaphoron*—it's neither here nor there, "for 'the earth and its fullness are the Lord's'" (1 Corinthians 10:26, referring to Psalm 24:1). But *how* one uses one's freedom to eat or not eat is everything.

And here's where chapter 9 becomes so important. Sometimes people read chapters 8–10 and see chapter 9 as some kind of weird digression where Paul goes off on a rabbit trail about himself and other apostles, since both chapters 8 and 10 mention idol meat and 9 does not. But chapter 9 is the linchpin of it all because there Paul gives concrete examples from his own life about the principle of using our liberty/authority [*exousia*] not to prove how free we are or puff ourselves up but to build others up. I will return to a modern example of this later. First, let's see how Paul models ethical Christian behavior for his congregation.

The Crucial "Nevertheless" (1 Corinthians 9)

At the end of chapter 8 Paul is talking about idol meat, and then he turns to his role as an apostle. What's the connection? In chapter 9, Paul models for the strong Corinthians what it looks like to set aside the self-centered ego and use one's power/status/liberty [*exousia*] for others to lead them into wholeness and healing [*sōzō*, often translated as "salvation" in English]. Often, the most powerful way to teach another person is to model by example what you want them to learn. Paul marches through all of the freedoms [*eleutheria*] and rights/liberty/authority [*exousia* gets translated all these ways] that he has as an apostle, including the right to a wife (yes, other apostles were married, including Peter, according to 1 Corinthians 9:5). He has the right to financial support to pay his bills, and he quotes Scripture to prove it.

The main point comes out in the middle of verse 12 with one little word that changes everything: "nevertheless" [*all' ouk* in Greek]: "*Nevertheless*, we have not made use of this right [*exousia*], but we endure anything rather than put an obstacle in the way of the gospel of Christ" (1 Corinthians 9:12, emphasis added). Don't trip people and make them fall. Lift them up.

In case they still haven't understood (let's face it, difficult or new truths require repetition), he again lists more rights [*exousia*] that he has and then at 9:15 again shows himself setting those rights aside for them and anyone else he can lift up, make whole, save [*sōzō*]. It's important to mention that since the Corinthians were so spiritually immature, Paul dared not take monetary support from them while he was trying to teach them truth so that there was no confusion about motives.

In contrast, you will see a congregation like the one in Philippi, full of mature Christians, that understands that those called to ministry still have to pay their bills and that ministering to the world actually costs money, and they cheerfully and joyfully and generously support Paul and others in sharing the gospel. They fund his missions to a dizzying array of places (if you ever do an "In the Footsteps of Paul" trip, you will get a real sense of this fact). Heck, who wouldn't rather merely provide some money, food, lodging, and clothing instead of being the one getting shipwrecked, beaten up, sick with fever, imprisoned, and so on? He still puts before the Corinthians, however, the fact that he is certainly entitled to pay, though in their case he forgoes it: "What then is my reward? Just this: that in my proclamation I may make the gospel free of charge, so as not to make full use of my rights [*exousia*] in the gospel" (1 Corinthians 9:18).

And why on earth would he do such a thing—laying aside his God-given rights, the freedom he has through Jesus to eat whatever he wants, from idol meat (relevant to the pagan context) to oysters and cheeseburgers (relevant to a Jewish context where both shellfish and mixing meat and dairy are not kosher)? Along with 1 Corinthians 9:12, 9:19-23 demonstrates succinctly what the Logic of the Cross looks like for Paul: "For though I am free with respect to all, I have made myself a slave to all. . . . I have become all things to all people, that I might by all means save some. I do it all for the sake of the gospel, so that I may share in its blessings." Paul invites the Corinthians, and us, to go and do likewise.

How Might This Look in Our Own Context?

Wear Pantyhose

Some people see Paul's "chameleon for Christ" approach as wishy-washy or not respectable, but that's an unfair accusation. First, if you follow Paul's writings, his life, and his death (he dies a martyr's death), he is anything but wishy-washy—he is a man of bedrock conviction when it comes to the grace offered through Jesus Christ. He's not wishy-washy; he's *discerning*. Paul is skilled at distinguishing what matters and what doesn't when it comes to practicing our faith. Paul is trained in Stoic philosophy, which teaches us that there are many things that are really neither here nor there (*adiaphoron*) when it comes down to it. You can see this reasoning in 1 Corinthians 7:19; Galatians 5:6; 6:15.

I served as an interim minister in a church in the Northeast back in the '90s. I was young then and the congregation was on the older side. I had to decide how I would dress to be seen as professional. Now, you can ask my mom, I am no fan of pantyhose—I can give you lots of reasons. True story: on the day of my wedding, standing in the narthex waiting to go into the sanctuary, I was squirming and complaining about the pantyhose I had on. My mom, quite "over" everything related to the wedding by then, I'm sure, but definitely over the pantyhose whining, reached up under my gown and yanked off the pantyhose, threw them in the little wastebasket sitting there, and bellowed: "Now, go in there and *get married*!" I really don't like pantyhose.

Nevertheless, I decided that the context called for skirts and pantyhose since what I wanted most was to be nonthreatening and someone the church could take seriously when it came to leading worship and marrying and burying people. Did I have the right to not wear pantyhose? Yes. Were pantyhose annoying and stupid and expensive? Yes. Were they a hill to die on? No. If wearing pantyhose could allow people to hear the content of my sermons and trust that I took the office of pastor seriously, then so be it. It was an *adiaphoron*. I thought about the Logic of the Cross, and I discerned that Jesus and Paul would have both chosen to wear pantyhose. So I did too.

A word of caution may be in order here. Let's not misread Paul's call to accommodate the needs of others or set aside one's authority or rights or not make a mountain out of a molehill as a call to become a doormat, letting people walk all over us, having no strong sense of self or boundaries. I assure you Paul never lost sight of who he was and what he stood for, and he courageously spoke his truth consistently with boldness and conviction, like Jesus before him. Paul is talking about things that we make a big deal out of and that cause fights and divisions unnecessarily (contemporary worship or traditional; abstinence from certain food or drinks). I would not lump in with this such issues as gender equality, racial justice, care of God's creation,

---

The Logic of the Cross asks us not to puff out our chests in a display of power but rather to ask what's best for the common good, most especially the most vulnerable among us.

LGBTQIA+ inclusion, or other profound issues involving the treatment of persons for whom Christ died. Of course, the church in every generation has to faithfully try to discern what counts as *adiaphora* vs. what is bedrock essential. Fortunately, we have all of the resources we need to do that.

To Mask or Not to Mask?

On a much more serious level than pantyhose, I'm writing during the 2020 COVID-19 pandemic. Certainly, we have seen a mix of behaviors driven by fear and anxiety (hoarding toilet paper and other supplies) as well as those motivated by kindness and compassion. We have also seen behavior that is ego-driven and sounds like a page from the Corinthian *pneumatikoi* playbook: "All things are lawful for me." We have seen this play out regarding choices related to social distancing and wearing masks.

In the first days of hearing about the virus, I had to decide whether I should cancel an international trip to do a lecture series in a country I've always wanted to visit. I was sharing the dilemma with a friend, noting that I am a healthy person who would probably be okay if I got it. She responded, "It's not about you. I'm seventy-one, and they've proven that if someone my age gets the virus, it can be a death sentence." I didn't realize my friend was that old, actually, and I said so. She responded: "It doesn't matter whether or not I *look* or *seem* like I'm seventy-one—I am. So when you make your choice, don't just think about yourself; consider the well-being of the more vulnerable." I canceled the trip as soon as I got home that night. The Logic of the Cross asks us not to puff out our chests in a display of power but rather to ask what's best for the common good, most especially the most vulnerable among us.

We are all in this together; we are interdependent; we are all important. May our actions reflect that.

Develop Skills and Habits of Mindfulness, Humility, and Compassion

Finally, if we are going to become all things to all people so that we might share the good news of healing and wholeness for all of God's creation, we will want to gain the skills and habits of mindfulness, humility, and compassion (literally "to suffer with"). Paul had to call the Corinthians away from the boasting, the being puffed up, and the competitive factionalism and toward community and connection. Over and over again, chapter after chapter, letter after letter (remember, it goes on into 2 Corinthians), he repeats the same lessons. They try to separate themselves and create hierarchies and pride themselves on their knowledge while disdaining others. But Paul calls them to compassion and connection, even for those who are less knowledgeable or make poor choices that require some intervention to contain destruction. This can be easier said than done sometimes (okay, a lot of times).

Paul became all things to all people in order that he might save some. When Paul looked upon a person who was weak or ignorant, he saw a person, no, a *family member*, for whom Christ died. How was Paul able to do this? By having the mind of Christ, by knowing that Christ was alive in Paul's being and that he was equipped with the Spirit of Christ to choose the path of compassion and connection. To do this he left behind his old ways of scratching his way to the top and preening about his accomplishments (Philippians 3:4-6) and of judging others to be so wrong that he "violently persecuted" and tried to destroy the church (1 Corinthians 15:9;

Galatians 1:13; Philippians 3:6). Paul changed and grew and became the leader God intended him to be. So can we.

Bob Johansen is a futurist who works in Silicon Valley and consults with some of the biggest movers and shakers in the world and has for decades. In his 2017 book *The New Leadership Literacies: Thriving in a Future of Extreme Disruption and Distributed Everything*, I was struck by the number of times "humility" came up as an important leadership quality. For example, read the following quotations about leadership in the future: "Enduring leadership qualities like strength, humility, and trust will still be foundational."[2] "Rock-star leaders will be rare; networked leadership with strength and humility will work best."[3] "Both humility and humor are important aspects of leadership."[4] "The literacy of creating and sustaining positive energy will require quiet transparency with strength, humility and empathy."[5]

We don't become more humble, compassionate, and connected with others, however, just by reading about it (trust me, I've tried); that kind of knowledge doesn't bear nourishing fruit. The "necessary knowledge" of which Paul speaks comes through *intentional practice*. Christian community is a primary place we learn and practice and develop these skills and habits and virtues. Many of us also take advantage of other resources as well, Christian or otherwise. We use the Enneagram for spiritual development, go on retreats to learn more about Nonviolent Communication (NVC), or learn from other trusted teachers and guides, like Brené Brown or Richard Rohr or the Dalai Lama or John Lewis—all of these can help us practice the love that Jesus and Paul teach about.

One such helpful teacher and guide is Tara Brach. Her hope-inducing words indicate not only that we should grow in mindfulness, humility, and compassion, but that we most certainly can. In her book *Radical Compassion*, Tara Brach writes,

> From an evolutionary perspective, our species' brain development correlates with a growing capacity for

> self-awareness, rational thinking, empathy, compassion, and mindfulness. No question, our very human fears and grasping, combined with our cognitive ability, also make us the greatest danger on earth to ourselves and all other species. But we are not at the end of our evolutionary story. We have the tools that can awaken mindfulness and compassion in ourselves and guide us in relating wisely and lovingly with others. . . . Radical compassion expresses the truth of our interdependence and mutual belonging. Living true to ourselves becomes, in its fullness, living true to our collective path of healing and freedom, our shared yearning for a peaceful, loving world.[6]

This last sentence sounds like a paraphrase of Paul's own view on our life in community. Paul summarizes well the whole long discussion in chapters 8–10 with these words: "So, whether you eat or drink, or whatever you do, do everything for the glory of God. Give no offense to Jews or to Greeks or to the church of God, just as I try to please everyone in everything I do, not seeking my own advantage, but that of many, so that they may be saved. Be imitators of me, as I am of Christ" (1 Corinthians 10:31–11:1).

Paul doesn't boastfully put himself forward as a model; rather he calls the Corinthian Christians to imitate him *insofar as he imitates Christ*. We all need teachers and mentors who model virtue for us just as we, in turn, find ways to encourage those who come behind us. At our best we do everything for the glory of God so that we might be agents of healing and wholeness just as we have been recipients.

CHAPTER 4

GATHERING FOR GOOD

In 1 Corinthians 11–14, Paul addresses problems that arise when the Corinthians gather together (which they did at least weekly, according to 16:2). At 11:17 he even says that the damage they cause when gathering is worse than if they didn't meet at all! What can we learn from them so that the same will never be said of us?

The "presenting problems" include the following:

1. whether or not women and men should wear hats in church when they prophesy;
2. how the Corinthians are bringing their habitual, hindering hierarchies to the Lord's Table; and
3. using spiritual gifts to puff up oneself instead of build up the community.

Recall that in chapters 8–10 Paul was dealing with one very specific issue, idol meat. In chapter 9 he focused on the foundational point of using one's *exousia* (authority/power/rights) for the sake of the greater good (the idol-meat example was just one manifestation of the deeper issue). The same kind of thing happens in chapters 11–14—in the middle of dealing with these specific problems that the Corinthians are fighting about, Paul pens 1 Corinthians 13, one of the most glorious texts ever composed. There he boils all of the specific issues down, once again, to love, since love is, after all, the fundamental Logic of the Cross. See how it is with God, Jesus, and Paul? It always comes down to love.

Hair That Praises Jesus? (1 Corinthians 11:1-16; 14:33b-36)

The first issue Paul discusses is whether or not men and women should cover their heads when prophesying in church. Some Christian traditions still find women wearing hats, habits, bonnets, or other head coverings, while strictly forbidding men to wear hats in a sanctuary. In fact, this comes up at our seminary graduation every year since it's held in a sanctuary. The female faculty are busy trying to pin their mortar-boards or tams to their puffy hair while the men wear them into the sanctuary and promptly take them off. Recently, there's been a movement for the women not to wear the coverings either since it seems silly to have different rules for different genders at an institution that is clearly committed to gender equality. These issues must be considered anew in each generation, not because one way is right and one is wrong but because the *meaning* that is implied by our practices can change over time.

A few preparatory comments before we look at some of the details in the text. First, space doesn't permit an extensive treatment of the passage. For a fuller exploration, see my chapter on Paul in *Women in the Bible*.[1] Second, though the argument gets dense in 11:1-16, pay attention to these two takeaways we learn: (1) we are called to do church in a creative, inclusive, interdependent way, and (2) women lead in Pauline churches.

Notice right away that the issue is not *whether* a woman should prophesy in church or not (1 Corinthians 11:5). Paul assumes both genders (two genders was all he knew about in the first century since they knew nothing about chromosomes, DNA, and so on) fill the same roles in gathered worship, and that includes prophesying. The issue instead is a cultural one—how everyone should dress. Why does he care? Because as always he is motivated first and foremost by inviting non-Christians into the faith. He thinks worship needs to be conducted in a way that highlights the distinctive values of Jesus. Outsiders should be able to come in, understand what is going on to a reasonable extent, be able to follow along (this is the problem with tongues, by the way, when they are not interpreted), and feel invited to join the Christian family.

To understand what Paul is actually getting at with head coverings, you need a few pieces of historical information. First, Paul says men should not cover their heads during worship and women should. This may sound confusing to those who know that modern Jewish men cover their heads with a *kipah* (in Yiddish, *yarmulke*). But that practice started after the New Testament period, which is to say today's custom for Jewish men is the exact opposite of that of the first century. On the other hand, Roman and Jewish women covered their heads. Uncovering a woman's head (or shaving it) was a punishing, shaming act. When one combines ancient cultural practice along with ancient views of gender and biology and "medicine," one learns that the ancients thought some strange things about men and women—especially women. The practice is to cover the head. The question one wonders about is why. To keep it simple, let's just say a woman's head was seen as needing to be protected from penetration.[2] The idea is to protect women from "illegitimate" penetration from any angle.

In addition to these ancient ideas about gender, it's also important to know that women who were associated with particular pagan cults (like mantic prophetesses or the Oracle of Delphi), wore their hair down and flowing. Paul wanted to distinguish the Christians from such cults. Finally, recall that he wanted the Corinthians to discern between the *adiaphora* (inconsequential, "neither-here-nor-there" things) from what really matters. Women covering their heads and men not doing so was one of those for Paul. This is a man who, upon baptizing congregants, declared,

In Christ, "there is no longer male and female" (Galatians 3:28). Christian Corinthians already knew this, but non-Christian ones didn't yet, and they wouldn't have a chance to if they would be too freaked out by what they saw the first time they attend a service. Hats, pantyhose—not a hill to die on.

The main thing is presenting the message of the gospel, and once people actually understand the cross, they, too, will be able to distinguish between what's essential (love) and what's not (hats and pantyhose).

As for the actual granular-level detailed argument that Paul presents, Wayne Meeks has wisely opined: "These are not the most lucid passages in the Pauline letters, and a small mountain of literature about them has by no means relieved their obscurity."[3] Let me highlight a few prominent points.

First, Paul begins by exhorting the Corinthians to "be imitators of me, as I am of Christ" (11:1; compare 4:16). What does he mean by that? Use your authority/rights [*exousia*] to do whatever it takes to spread the gospel in the short time remaining. It's the same argument we saw in our treatment of 1 Corinthians 8–10.

Second, let's outline the "argument." In 11:3-8, Paul appears to subordinate women to men. The salient moves in this section of the argument include: (1) a woman should have long hair and a veil; she should not have short hair or a shaved head; (2) a man should have short hair and no veil; and (3) woman was made from man, not vice versa. One immediately notices that Paul has eclipsed the first Creation story, which states, "So God created humankind in his image, / in the image of God he created them; / male and female he created them" (Genesis 1:27), and invoked only the second Creation story (Genesis 2).

However, Paul then gives women back power and levels the playing field. He moves directly to the *exousia* argument, granting that women have authority [*exousia*] over their own heads (1 Corinthians 11:10), just as Paul has *exousia* associated with being an apostle, the "strong" in chapters 8–10 have *exousia* over food, and so on. Then he says, "nevertheless," which indicates a contrast with what has come before: "Nevertheless, in the Lord woman is not independent of man or man independent of woman. For just as woman came from man, so man comes through woman; but all things come from God" (11:11-12). That is, though he has made a number of comments that might lead some to subordinate women, Paul stops that trajectory. In the church (here "in the Lord"), things are done differently. Interdependently.

First Corinthians 11:11-12, like Galatians 3:28, defies "arguments for female subordination that depend on the second creation story."[4] From the cross, we learn to reject systems of domination and relish interdependence, knowing that abundant life depends upon it. We will see this again in the next chapter with the body metaphor Paul uses.

In the following verses (1 Corinthians 11:13-15),

> Paul argues that nature itself supports the idea of a woman veiling: "Judge for yourselves: is it proper for a woman to pray to God with her head unveiled? Does not nature itself teach you that if a man wears long hair, it is degrading to him, but if a woman has long hair, it is her glory? For her hair is given to her for a covering." Two points should be made. First is the obvious point that nature does not teach this. Culture does. Second, this is not about subordination of women. It's simply about the cultural customs related to head covering while the women are praying in church.[5]

We have our own cultural customs around hair and head coverings. When teaching verses 2-16 to groups, I ask participants to talk to me about hairstyles and how they relate to social class, professional status, social status, religion, ethnicity, and so on.

> One can discern an expensive color job from an inexpensive one, an expensive weave from a cheap one. Hair with purple and orange streaks may work for an

> artist but not for a Supreme Court judge. Even these few examples highlight [pardon the pun] that how one wears one's hair (or whether one's hair is even showing) is often a sign of culture and status today. And sometimes our cultural assumptions about hair can be harmful to women. Consider Chris Rock's movie *Good Hair*. He made the movie in response to his four-year-old daughter's question: "Daddy, why don't I have good hair?" Early on she had learned that African American hair is not "good hair." Many interesting, helpful conversations about race, ethnicity, and culture have arisen as groups discuss hair, status, gender, culture, and power gathered around [this passage].[6]

Of course in Corinth women are praying and prophesying in church, since they serve in the same roles as men throughout Paul's ministry. The particular Corinthian context called for women to cover their heads while leading, just as it called for the men to wear their hair short and uncovered. Today, of course, our culture has different customs surrounding hair, just as every culture does: for example, in the United States we see some male pastors wearing their hair long. In addition, most images I see of Jesus in churches depict him with long hair!

I can't resist telling you the story of debating Paul's statement that "nature" teaches that men have short hair. Eventually someone brought up Jesus and his hair. Exasperated, one very short-haired male in the class blurted out: "Look, people, Paul saw Jesus himself on the road to Damascus. I think he knows if Jesus had long or short hair" (implying Jesus had short hair, given Paul's ruling). When you picture Jesus, what kind of hair does he have (and, for that matter, what color skin, eyes, and so on)? Where do you think you derived your image from? What difference does it make for you to picture Jesus's features one way or another?

Hair is a culturally significant phenomenon in every culture.

But What About 1 Corinthians 14:33b-36?

In 1 Corinthians 14, Paul is wrapping up the unit devoted to orderly worship that began at 11:1. In the middle of his talking about speaking in tongues and how that relates to prophesying, the argument is interrupted by a statement about women (14:33b-36). Your study Bible puts it in parentheses to mark it as an odd intrusion. The statement directly contradicts what we find not only in the rest of Paul's letters and practice (women leaders in the churches, Galatians 3:28, and so on) but also just three chapters earlier in 1 Corinthians 11, where Paul assumes that women both pray and prophesy in the church. As we saw there, the question has nothing to do with *whether* they speak in church—they clearly do—(it doesn't make any sense, of course, to prophesy at home by yourself) but whether or not they wear a head covering *while doing so*.

Because of these other things we know about Paul, it's not surprising that most scholars don't think that Paul wrote 14:33b-36. Scholars debate the authenticity of the passage for a number of reasons. First, it interrupts the argument; if one removes it, the passage continues to flow in its discussion of tongues and prophecy.

Second, because the passage sounds strikingly parallel to 1 Timothy 2:11-15, many scholars take 1 Corinthians 14:33b-36 to be a harmonizing scribal interpolation. Remember, these texts were all copied by hand by scribes. Since scribes knew other texts, at times one text would remind them of another, and they might note that in the margin. Or, in an effort to clarify or deepen the meaning of a passage (in their estimation), they might harmonize one text with another (this is how we came to have numerous endings to the Gospel of Mark, for example). Even though our manuscripts don't omit the passage, they do place some of the verses in different places. This further suggests the scribal gloss theory. If you are truly interested in how you got the Bible in your hands, including understanding scribal practices, read *The Text of the New Testament* by Bart Ehrman and Bruce Metzger.

Third, this passage contradicts the witness of Paul's own ministry as demonstrated across his letters, which shows women as leaders in the churches. If Paul did write the passage, he can't have meant that women should be entirely silent. Or, perhaps more importantly, whatever he meant by them, the way he put these words into practice meant something very different from the way people have interpreted them today, which is to limit women's leadership.

Who Wore It Best? Trying It On for Size, Gospel-Style

Paul concludes the whole worship unit, chapters 11–14, with these summarizing words: "So, my friends, be eager to prophesy, and do not forbid speaking in tongues; but all things should be done decently and in order" (1 Corinthians 14:39-40). Since the purpose of this study is to get a sense of 1 Corinthians as a whole and why and how it might be relevant to our own context, here are three points related to our review of 11:1-16 and 14:33b-36:

1. Women exercise authority in the church as followers of Christ, just as men do. To use 1 Corinthians to "keep women in their place" is to misread the text.
2. Ancient head coverings are like modern pantyhose—an *adiaphoron* (neither here nor there). Don't let superficial cultural conventions hinder the proclamation of the gospel. If it's not a big deal, don't make it a big deal. On the other hand, don't stand down on issues that *are* a big deal. Learn to discern. When possible, kindly work to stretch the horizons and capacities of those who are confusing the essential with the nonessential.
3. Just as we saw in 1 Corinthians 7, Paul insists that people of all genders are interdependent. In fact, we are all interdependent, regardless of race, class, gender, education level, nationality, and

so on. We are all in this together, folks. We are saved together or we are damned together. Paul is a Jew, a member of a covenant people. No biblical author, from Genesis to Revelation, imagined the idea of a committed follower of God who was not part of a *community*, as messy as that has always been and always will be. Being in community means balancing convictions with concessions; hence the need to develop the virtues of compassion, maturity, and the kind of love Paul presents in 1 Corinthians 13. It's not just a pretty poem—it's our Christian calling.

The Lord's Supper: Table Manners and the Power of Pre-eating (1 Corinthians 11:17-34)

I have a fabulously fun, smart, witty friend who usually eats dinner early, such that when we are going out in a group at a later time, he is ravenous and distracted by hunger by the time we are served (and thus, not his best, most engaging self that we normally expect). So we now get him to "pre-eat"—a bowl of cereal, a protein bar, whatever works. Never, however, has his peckishness caused the kind of ruckus we see in 1 Corinthians 11:17-34!

What's going on here that has Paul all knotted up? We're back to divisions, in this case between rich and poor. Once again, the Corinthians have been sucked into the frenetic rat race and have momentarily forgotten the liberating Logic of the Cross. The church is *supposed to* gather as a community, eat, and share the Lord's Supper, modeling for the world that God considers each and every person as equally valuable, thus modeling the baptismal proclamation of Galatians 3:28. They are invited to live on earth as it is in heaven.

What's *actually* happening is that when they gather they conduct business as usual; if you walked in, it would look like any other gathering in the imperial world: the wealthier Christians take the best seats, and they eat and drink the best portions—way more than they need or is good for them—while the poorer Christians wait for the crumbs and leftovers, expecting little and getting little, as per usual. Nothing remarkable. Ostensibly, this is "just how the world works." The wealthy get the seats of honor and take the good stuff. The poor get the leftovers, if they're lucky. Everyone's acting out their "assigned role" in the social hierarchy that has supposedly been ordained since "time immemorial," supposedly by "the gods/nature/God" but in reality only by human beings like Aristotle, the emperor, and other sadly deluded power brokers in church and state.

The God of Jesus Christ has not ordained such nonsense. And therein lies the issue. Paul directly confronts the class stratification and reminds them all that they come together in the name of Jesus Christ, who exploded those hierarchies to bits. Anything they have is a gift from God to be shared and used for the building up of the community. If the jetsetters are so hungry that they make the Lord's Supper their personal Las Vegas–style buffet, then they need to start pre-eating before they arrive at the gathering and let the poorer people get their fill at the gathering. Read Paul's exact words: "So then, my brothers and sisters, when you come together to eat, wait for one another. If you are hungry, eat at home, so that when you come together, it will not be for your condemnation" (1 Corinthians 11:33-34).

It's back to the same issue we've seen all along. Yes, you are really special, and you have freedom and authority and success. To have the mind of Christ, however, to become spiritually mature, means to share all of that to build up others, to invite them to experience abundance. Paul's words in the idol-meat controversy hold true in this situation as well, where the strong (here those with material abundance) are lording it over the weak (here those who are less affluent). There it was, "So by your knowledge

Signing on with Jesus means committing to a community of people that includes folks you might not otherwise come across in your daily life.

those weak believers for whom Christ died are destroyed. But when you thus sin against members of your family, and wound their conscience when it is weak, you sin against Christ" (8:11-12). In this case he says, "What! Do you not have homes to eat and drink in? Or do you show contempt for the church of God and humiliate those who have nothing? What should I say to you? Should I commend you? In this matter I do not commend you!" (11:22). In effect, he says, "Jesus died for these people. The least you can do is pre-eat."

To be fair, what Paul is saying is mind-boggling in their context, and, let's be honest, our own. To *say* that the poorest slave has the same amount of honor and value as the richest landowner—let alone *behave* as if it's true—goes against the grain. Unless that grain is the body of Christ, given for all of them, and the cup is the new covenant in his blood. If that's the case, then gathering in name of Jesus (instead of say, the current head of state or Dionysius or Roma or Mithras or any other idol) will look a lot different than business as usual. Who ever heard of a divine being giving of themselves in sacrificial love, gladly spending and being spent on the beloved rather than basking in ego and power? Revolutionary love.

Following this God means seriously loving and committing to your neighbor as if they were Christ, since Christ lives in them. This is not a religion where you pay homage to the god for whatever ails you in a kind of bartering transaction, and then you get stuff. Signing on with Jesus means committing to a community of people that includes folks you might not otherwise come across in your daily life or might not consider equal to you and probably never felt a responsibility for before. How we interact with our neighbor matters to God. Reread verses 27-29. The reference to the "body" here is a reference to the gathered body of Christ—the church (as we will see in more detail in 1 Corinthians 12). It's not an individualistic thing—at every turn from 1 Corinthians 1 to the end, Paul keeps repeating the point about how we treat one another:

- Don't eat the idol meat in front of people who will be freaked out by it.
- Protect the lives of other people, even if it inconveniences you (as in our present-day pandemic).
- Pre-eat.

It is no small thing to humiliate poorer brothers and sisters, to assume that they should be grateful for the crumbs that fall off our table. We are all guests at the Lord's Table. There is only one host, and it's not you, me, or your pastor.

Notice that Paul speaks in the second person plural throughout (y'all), and verses like 22 show Paul again speaking a particularly strong word to the "strong," the ones higher up on the social ladder of education, money, power, and status. They are the ones in the position to change the situation. As Jesus himself said, "To whom much has been given, much will be required" (Luke 12:48).

How does all of this play out in our modern context? How do we conduct *agape* meals or the Lord's Supper (Communion, Eucharist)? Are we wildly extravagant and inviting? Are all bodies equally valued, equally served, equally included? Using Paul's more austere language, are we showing contempt or humiliating certain people? What about people with disabilities, cognitive or physical? People who are poor? People across genders? Jesus has made it clear that this table has inexhaustible sustenance. Let's celebrate the joy and nourishment we find at Jesus's table and ask ourselves if we're making it accessible to all.

Consider something as "simple" as offering gluten-free bread for Communion to be inclusive of those who can't eat wheat, rye, or barley. Although well intentioned, I've seen this go wrong in a number of ways:

1. The bread offered is gluten free but the cup has chunks of regular bread in it.
2. The gluten-free bread is on the same plate as the regular bread.
3. There are different stations set up, so there's regular bread at some stations and then a gluten-free option at one station. Thus, a person has to be publicly singled out about a personal medical condition.

The solution may be to serve gluten-free bread to all of us (though GF bread still can contain eggs and some people have egg allergies). The same would hold true for serving only grape juice, given that some people cannot drink alcohol. *The point is,* can we listen to the real-life facts of every embodied person and then make choices that are inclusive of all of us? If you start to feel like it's "too much trouble" or "over-the-top" to attend to the real bodies who show up in your community, it might be good to ask *why* it feels annoying or exasperating rather than an exciting, relatively easy opportunity to signal and participate in the abundant love of God who cherishes each and every person and knows us by name. How do our shared practices reflect God's delight in the presence of each and every one of God's unique children at the table instead of "one more problem or inconvenience to be overcome to get through the Sunday service"?

This change was made in one church I was in, and I was encouraged by that. During one of our phases of collecting feedback, one person said: "Bring back our sourdough Communion bread!" Some people in the room laughed and agreed. I found myself thinking about two things. First, 1 Corinthians, as we've been discussing it here. Second, I had just finished teaching a course on the Gospel of John in which one of my brilliant students, Rev. Jennifer Logsdon-Kellogg, who suffers from celiac disease, wrote a powerful poem and a one-page explanation of it for a final. While the poem was motivated by Jesus's Bread from Heaven Discourse in John 6, it was and is relevant to the issue of why demanding sourdough bread for Communion falls short of imitating Christ.

I wrote to the pastoral staff at the time (two people I respect and admire) to say I'd been sitting with the request for the sourdough bread to be brought back for Communion. I shared that if this arose in my class setting, I would have the class read 1 Corinthians 11 about the Lord's Supper, where Paul discusses "discerning the body" (referring to the church, the body of Christ). Paul takes seriously, of course, making concessions for the sake of our brothers and sisters. He tells them that the meal isn't about them and that if it's their bellies they are most worried about (or taste buds) they can just pre-eat at home before they come to the table. I would then remind them of 1 Corinthians 8–10 and the idol-meat controversy, where Paul, who likes meat and can eat it, nonetheless declares that his choices should be dictated by what is best for the person who needs a concession (not that folks who can't eat gluten are "weak," of course, but it's the same idea): "Therefore, if food is a cause of their falling, I will never eat meat, so that I may not cause one of them to fall" (8:13).

Then there's Romans 12, where Paul calls us to humility and to recall that we are all connected to one another. And there's Jesus's call to love your neighbor as yourself (Mark 12:31 citing Leviticus 19:18)—I assume if we *all* had celiac disease or intolerances to gluten, it would be easier for us to love our neighbor as ourselves when it comes to this.

Here's the poem I referred to by Rev. Logsdon-Kellogg. I include her poem here in hopes it can help other churches consider how to become more Christlike at the Communion table.

Body of Christ Given—

"The body of Christ given—"
"I can't eat the bread."
hands closed. arms crossed.
Weirdo.
The bread of life?
Not. For Me.

"Can you give me a blessing instead?"
Is this not the international sign
Meaning 'bless me'?
Apparently not.

Confused Silence.
Rejection based on ignorance is still
. . . rejection.

"I can't eat the bread.
Can you give me a blessing, instead?"

The true bread.
The living bread. The bread
for the life of the universe.
Eat this bread, savor it—
and **Jesus** will happen to you.
This sweet round Hawaiian loaf from heaven
taken, blessed, broken and given to all—

"I can't eat the bread."
to all but me.
"Can you give me a blessing . . . instead?"

"Well we have these crackers . . ."
On the same plate with the bread crumbs
that may as well be poison
To dip in the cup with Hawaiian bread
floating.

"Take this bread."

"Amen." So be it.
Maybe it won't hurt too long. 3 days? 4?
But I do want Jesus.
"The cup of blessing."
"Amen." *Omigod the cracker's moldy.*
Can't spit Jesus out.

Kneel at the rail and choke
—on tears.

"Do you want to be well?"
I want to be *fed*. From
One body
One loaf.
In union: communion.
To share with my church
The true bread from heaven.

Without causing a spectacle in the
communion line—
and still getting glutened anyway.

"I can't eat *this* bread.
Can you give me a blessing instead?
... Use different bread?"

"But it's messy..."
"But we've always..."
"But it's expensive..."

Water into wine
Five loaves for five thousand
153 fish—
Jesus feeds abundantly.

"Love each other as I have loved
you," Jesus said.

"I AM the bread."[7]

Used by permission.

In her reflection on the poem, Logsdon-Kellogg writes,

> Celiac disease is an autoimmune condition that causes your immune system to go to war against wheat, barley, and rye. A few crumbs of bread, like one might get via communion by intinction from a cup that has already had gluten-filled bread dipped in it, could cause short-term misery as well as long-term physical damage for someone with celiac. The poem reflects my raw experience—feelings of deep rejection from my own church at the communion table. The point of communion is union. For people to be treated as "other" when they physically cannot eat the bread of unity is a theological problem, not simply a logistical one. The shared loaf is important.
>
> The poem is meant to prompt questions: Whom is Jesus drawing to himself, to the table, to the church?[8]

If our church responds faithfully to such questions, we might find ourselves entertaining angels unawares, maybe even a Sara Miles. In her compelling memoir, *Take This Bread,* Miles tells the story of when she decided on impulse one day to walk into a church: "I had no earthly reason to be there. I'd never heard a Gospel reading, never said the Lord's Prayer. I was certainly not interested in becoming a Christian—or, as I thought of it rather less politely, a religious nut. . . . I went in, on an impulse, with no more than a reporter's habitual curiosity." She describes the service, including the Lord's Supper: "And then we gathered around that table. And there was more singing and standing, and someone was putting a piece of fresh, crumbly bread in my hands, saying 'the body of Christ,' and handing me the goblet of sweet wine, saying 'the blood of Christ,' and then something outrageous and terrifying happened. Jesus happened to me."[9]

I certainly enjoy both Hawaiian bread and sourdough, but I can eat it before or after church if I'm really craving it. It's an *adiaphoron.* Like the

---

What an exciting opportunity each and every church has to gather for good, using the talents and gifts of each person!

---

pantyhose, like the hats. Some problems are really easy to solve if we put on the mind of Christ and not confuse our *desires* with our *needs*.

Closing Thoughts

In this chapter we have explored the beauty and the challenges of creating Christian community that is faithful to the Jesus in whose name we gather in the first place. We hear Paul's call both to let the Holy Spirit loose (so, "do not forbid speaking in tongues" [1 Corinthians 14:39]) and to have a structure and order that allow the worship to be meaningful and accessible to every body gathered there (and I do mean every body, not just everybody). The Logic of the Cross insists that every body matters. And, in true Pauline/Jesus/God ironic fashion, it turns out that the very bodies devalued by the world's standards hold "greater" honor by God's standards. What an exciting opportunity each and every church has to gather for good, using the talents and gifts of each person! Let's dig deeper into that in the next chapter.

CHAPTER 5

TALENTED AND GIFTED

Where I live, the schools have special TAG programs. TAG stands for Talented and Gifted—as if those *not* chosen for the program are *not* talented and gifted. It's for children who are supposedly exceptionally "smart." It turns out that in some other states, that same designation applies to people who are considered cognitively impaired. This irony perfectly introduces the conversation about spiritual gifts in 1 Corinthians 12, which insists that we are all TAG and that our assumptions about hierarchies related to giftedness are ill-founded from God's perspective.

I have a friend who is deeply empathetic and nonjudgmental. She's been through a lot and courageously shares enough of her story in just such a way that it frees other people to open up to her about their own struggles in honest and vulnerable ways. I once wrote this comment to her: "You were *born* to be a safe space for people who could never imagine such a thing as 'safe space' for *them*. Others maybe, but not *them*. That's what we mean, in part, by a 'call' and a 'vocation.' It's a real thing. Often, people who have a particular call and vocation tend to assume that everyone else has those capacities, skills, and insights as well. They don't realize that they are special in that way. I hope you are understanding more and more that most of us don't share your capacities, skills, and insights. We are gifted in different ways but not in the ways that you come by as naturally as breathing air. This is why community and the image of the *body* of Christ is essential."

Spiritual Gifts (of Individuals and Communities) (1 Corinthians 12 and 14:1-33)

Chapter 12 marks something new and something old as Paul turns to the subject of spiritual gifts. We know it's a new topic (turning away from the instructions on the Lord's Supper) because it begins with the familiar *peri de,* "Now concerning. . . ." It's also an old topic since the point of the instruction is aimed at how those gifts are to be used for the common good, with Paul's ongoing themes of interdependence, unity in the Spirit, proper boasting (instead of false modesty or true arrogance), and, ultimately and always—love. Church is about community, according to Paul. In many ways, you don't come to the garden alone (though I do love the hymn) and even if you do tarry there while the dew is still on the roses, at the end of the hour, you are always called back to community. Paul writes, "To each is given the manifestation of the Spirit for the common good" (12:7). There is only one reason God has given each of us individual gifts—the edification [*oikodomeō*, building] of God's beloved community. We are better together and more than the sum of our parts.

I am awestruck and dumbstruck when it comes to spiritual gifts. I'm awestruck by the brilliance and varieties of gifts that I see in people of all places and ages. I am dumbstruck by the number of people who (a) don't recognize their gifts or (b) don't understand the value of their gifts for the wider world. This should remind us all how important it is both to discover our own gifts (we *all* have them) and to *name* the gifts of others and not just assume they know.

As a seminary professor with second-career students, I've been surprised and delighted to come across people who are finally living into their gifts or into another one of their gifts. One problem, honestly, is the sexism of the church that does not lift up and mentor women, people with

It's important to learn what gifts we bring to the table and pray about and learn about how they might best be used for the flourishing of all creation.

disabilities, and other minoritized people. For many of us, until someone takes us aside personally and names the gifts they see, we won't believe we have them. We will think, "Well, if I *were* gifted in this or that or called into ministry, *somebody* would have told me along the way." But others assume we already know our gifts and that it would be weird or presumptuous to name our gifts to us.

Jack Kornfield relates the powerful poignance of our gifts being named in his presentation "Seeing the Goodness in Another Being."[1] He tells the story of a teacher whose students had lost focus for that day. The teacher had each student write out what they appreciated about every other student in the class. Years later, one of those students died in combat in Afghanistan. It turns out that all those years, he had kept those comments with him in his wallet. The comments were mentioned by the student's mother after his funeral. It was discovered that day that many other students from the class had also saved their classmates' comments. If the phrase hadn't already been taken, I'd say "If you see something, say something" would be a good motto for identifying gifts.

Whether it's CliftonStrengths, the Enneagram, or some kind of spiritual gifts inventory, it's important to learn what gifts we bring to the table and pray about and learn about how they might best be used for the flourishing of all creation. Everyone has a spiritual gift; some people have multiple gifts. In chapter 12 Paul names some examples of gifts; it's a suggestive, not exhaustive, list. What would you add? Encouragement? Hospitality? Logistics? Praying with people? Artistic talent? Philanthropy?

Unity in Diversity: A Divine Creation

As we turn to a more detailed look at 1 Corinthians 12, I want you to notice a rhetorical technique that Paul (and other ancient authors) is very fond of; it's called *chiasm*. Using an A-B-A' structure, the author places special emphasis on the distinctive feature, B. In this chapter we have:

A: verses 1-11 Gifts

B: verses 12-26 The Body

A': verses 27-31 Gifts

The structure itself, in addition to the words, makes Paul's point—we are members of a body, not lone rangers, whose gifts are given to build the community of love. In fact, the structure of the whole unit of chapters 12–14 makes this point, since chapters 12 and 14 discuss gifts and the center, chapter 13, focuses on love. Thus, the gifts are for the purpose of building up love.

Chapter 12:1 reads *peri de tōn pneumatikōn*, which the NRSV translates as "Now concerning spiritual gifts...." I include the Greek here because *pneumatikōn* is a plural adjective, but its referent (the noun it modifies) is unclear due to an ambiguity in the Greek plural form, which could be masculine, feminine, or neuter. It might refer to spiritual gifts (though the word *gift, charisma,* would have to be supplied since it's not in the text there), or it might refer to "the things of the Spirit," or it might refer to people (those who consider themselves "spiritual"). Recall our discussion earlier of the *pneumatikoi* (the ones fancying themselves to be hyper-spiritual), whom we also called "the strong." Since we are now in chapter 12 and this is a pattern, it's reasonable to think he's still addressing those who are full of themselves (remember *physioō*, "puffed up," full of hot air?). Plus, there's no real reason to choose only one meaning—the ambiguity on Paul's part may be intentional. In this section of the letter, we find that some people seem to believe their gifts are superior to other people's. In addition, they seem to have forgotten that their gifts come from God—they did not earn them or create them—they merely received them.

Reread 1 Corinthians 12:4-6. Notice here that the word *gift* [*charisma*] *does* appear specifically. The word is best thought of as a "gift of grace" since the word for grace is in it—*charis*. Notice also the mention of all three members of the Trinity (the word *Trinity* never appears in the Bible): the Spirit, Christ (the Lord), and God. Diversity and unity, hand in hand. God-given diversity, by divine design that does not result in cacophony but rather symphony. This reemphasizes the point Paul made earlier about himself and Apollos, that the diversity is given by God and there is no reason for competition, boasting, or hierarchy: "What then is Apollos? What is Paul? Servants through whom you came to believe, as the Lord assigned to each. I planted, Apollos watered, but God gave the growth. So neither the one who plants nor the one who waters is anything, but only God who gives the growth" (1 Corinthians 3:5-7). He reiterates this in 4:6-7 also.

All along we have seen factions and hierarchies among the Corinthians that are completely "normal" and understandable in their context. In Roman society, certainly some people are more valued than others. We saw the fruits of this in the behavior at the Lord's Supper, where both the rich and poor donned their usual roles with the rich getting the first, best, and the most and the poor getting the seconds, worst, and least. But Paul keeps on trying to teach them the ironic logic of Jesus: the first shall be last, losing is gaining, turning the other cheek—all these values that directly contradict the "logic of the world." We see the same struggle here in chapter 12. Paul uses the wonderfully rich metaphor of the body to help his people understand what a church is and how people relate. We are the body of Christ (recall that just one chapter earlier Paul dealt with the body of Christ in terms of the Eucharist/Lord's Supper/Jesus's own body and the church—thus, the word *body* has three interrelated meanings in 1 Corinthians: Jesus's body, the church, and our individual body):

> *For just as the body is one and has many members, and all the members of the body, though many, are one body, so it is with Christ. For in the one Spirit we were all baptized into one body—Jews or Greeks, slaves or free—and we were all made to drink of one Spirit.*
>
> *Indeed, the body does not consist of one member but of many.*
>
> *1 Corinthians 12:12-14*

We all know that different body parts contribute differently to the working of a healthy body. Interdependence is fundamental; when one body part is affected, the whole body is affected. It's a beautiful, organic, dynamic metaphor. That is, until people start asking, "Yes, but who's the greatest?" The disciples asked it of Jesus repeatedly (Luke 9:46-48; 22:24-27), and he always gave the same ironic answer, some version of this:

> *"The kings of the Gentiles lord it over them; and those in authority over them are called benefactors. But not so with you; rather the greatest among you must become like the youngest, and the leader like one who serves. For who is greater, the one who is at the table or the one who serves? Is it not the one at the table? But I am among you as one who serves."*
>
> *Luke 22:25-27*

Paul takes the same approach, flip-flopping "normal" expectations of who is more valuable than whom:

> *The eye cannot say to the hand, "I have no need of you," nor again the head to the feet, "I have no need of you." On the contrary, the members of the body that seem to be weaker are indispensable, and those members of the body that we think less honorable we clothe with greater honor, and our less respectable members are treated with greater respect.*
>
> *1 Corinthians 12:21-23*

Paul clearly intends the metaphor to signal actual human bodies in the community, just as he does throughout the letter. It's yet another call for them to leave their learned biases at the door and take up Jesus's own perspective on how we view people (including children) and their value and how we best fit together to function most symbiotically and symphonically as Christ's body.

Whose Bodies Matter?

If Paul were to visit America in general and churches in America specifically, would he find disparities in the treatment of different bodies, some held in higher regard, treated with respect, clothed with honor, considered to be the most important part of the body? Who in our current society (and our churches) is considered less than, treated as less than? The Black Lives Matter movement and the Me Too movement have called direct attention to ways some members of the body politic (whether church or state), who hold the places of power and honor (the eye and the head), are saying, "We have no need of you" (to the hands and the feet). People with disabilities and immigrants experience this as well, and the message gets mapped onto their real flesh-and-blood bodies. How can Christians discern which members are being treated as disposable? And because Paul certainly demanded that the Christians change not just their ideas, but also their actions, and not in the future, but instantly, how do we bring to bear a Pauline practice of calling the powerful down and lifting the powerless or vulnerable up so that the whole body can function the way that God intended for this cosmos God created?

Over and over Paul practices what he preaches—we are all members of one body; that's the way God chose to do Creation. Paul spends his life becoming "all things to all people" so that they, too, could experience wholeness, salvation, reconciliation. He calls them to discern the same thing at the Lord's Supper—there's only one table, one meal. There is no "head table" or "special menu," and they eat together, all at the same time. Would Paul say that we are following his lead or not? Are we in the church adopting the Logic of the Cross, giving "greater honor" to those we usually consider "less honorable" and so on? Do we have "the same care for one another"? Does the following describe us or not: "If one member suffers, all suffer together with it"?

All of us are part of the one body. Thank God. Some of us are feet, and some of us are eyes. Some of us are tongues, apparently, or at least speak in tongues.

TAG Tongues?

It's no surprise, given the Corinthian context, that Paul explicitly mentions gifts of knowledge, wisdom, and speaking, since some people with those gifts are needing some extra instruction on how to use them. Recall that we highlighted the "thanksgiving portion" in 1 Corinthians 1:4-9 and said that one of the functions is to foreshadow the main points of the letter. There Paul said,

> *I give thanks to my God always for you because of the grace [*charis*] of God that has been given you in Christ Jesus, for in every way you have been enriched in him, in* speech *and* knowledge *of every kind—just as the testimony of Christ has been strengthened among you—so that you are not lacking in any spiritual gift [*charisma*] as you wait for the revealing of our Lord Jesus Christ.*
>
> *1 Corinthians 1:4-7, emphasis added*

You can see the connection: the Corinthians do indeed have gifts of speech and knowledge, but Paul's tone is a bit ironic insofar as he is going to have to school them in the proper, mature use of said gifts. Take the gift of tongues, for example; it is clearly one of the more visible gifts a person can have. Rather than debate the exact nature of the tongues, the point is that it is language not understood by others who are present. Paul himself has this gift amply (14:18), and it's a legitimate way to speak to God. Those who do so are "speaking mysteries in the Spirit" (14:2). Sounds great, right? So what's the problem? Why does he say that he prefers people to prophesy than to speak in tongues? There are two reasons, which are both "on-brand" for Paul.

First, as always, Paul is concerned to invite others into the faith. When the community gathers together for worship, we should assume there will be experienced Christians and non-Christian visitors and newbie Christians. If someone starts speaking in tongues and there is no one to interpret it, it's worse than pointless because it detracts from the worship experience because it is unintelligible to others and therefore uninviting. It builds up nothing but the ego of the one speaking, so it becomes show-offy, an example of an action that puffs up instead of builds up (1 Corinthians 14:4). The only exception is if there's someone there to interpret the tongues so that visitors can understand, be addressed by the gospel, and be invited to follow Jesus. Paul puts it this way:

> *If, therefore, the whole church comes together and all speak in tongues, and outsiders or unbelievers enter, will they not say that you are out of your mind? But if all prophesy, an unbeliever or outsider who enters is reproved by all and called to account by all. After the secrets of the unbeliever's heart are disclosed, that person will bow down before God and worship him, declaring, "God is really among you."*
>
> *1 Corinthians 14:23-25*

Second, notice that Paul doesn't want unbelievers to come to worship and think "these people are out of their minds." He's not a fan of "mindless Christianity" but rather *mindful* Christianity. Maybe you had a granny who used to tell you you'd better "mind" her, meaning behave appropriately. Paul agrees. But he is also a serious fan of gaining knowledge that matters (the kind that builds up others) and using whatever mind (and body, we'll get to that) you've been given. As Paul says in Romans 12:2, "be transformed by the renewing of your minds." Mindful Christians act *intentionally*, in accordance with the Logic of the Cross. They may or may not be educated, smart, or eloquent, but they are steeped in the soul-knowledge of cross-logic and intentional about choosing behaviors that show commitment to it.

Me and We

Consider the two times Paul lists out the gifts (at 1 Corinthians 12:8-11 and 28-30). We are specifically told that the Spirit gifts individuals however the Spirit so chooses. This raises some points to ponder.

First, it can be freeing to recognize that we have specific God-given strengths. Thus, we don't have to spend our lives lamenting the fact that we don't have some other kind of gift (as tempting as that can be). Second, we don't need to strive to be what we were not created to be (despite the trips our parents, mentors, or any number of people try to lay on us). I'm thinking here of the premise of the CliftonStrengths approach, which advises us against spending our time developing our areas of weakness. The authors write:

> Most organizations are built on two flawed assumptions about people:
>
> 1. Each person can learn to be competent in almost anything.
>
> 2. Each person's greatest room for growth is in his or her areas of greatest weakness.[2]

In contrast, "the two assumptions that guide the world's best managers" are the following:

> 1. Each person's talents are enduring and unique.
>
> 2. Each person's greatest room for growth is in the areas of his or her greatest strength.[3]

Serena Williams plays tennis; Yo-Yo Ma plays the cello; doctors perfect the ability to diagnose and heal; Neil Degrasse Tyson and Sean Carroll understand and teach us about the cosmos; Vera Wang designs gowns; Beyoncé sings; Meryl Streep acts; Ruth Bader Ginsburg adjudicated; Tina Fey makes us laugh; Queen Elizabeth II rules. Play to your strengths, and let the rest of us benefit from it.

Having said that, I'm a big fan of hobbies and avocations in my own life. Yes, I'm a professor of New Testament—that's my clear calling and joy. But I also go through phases of trying on something new for fun, with no regard for talent or giftedness. It's fun, rejuvenating, and interesting for a time, and then I move on. But my hobbies are not the same as my vocation.

One could argue that the same holds true for churches. Instead of trying to excel in every gift, perhaps churches need to discern their particular strengths in any given era and match the strengths of the church with those who can be best served by those strengths.

Mystical Experiences

Losing oneself in ecstatic mystical experiences is holy, beautiful, and true and a firmly established part of our Christian tradition, whether it's through singing hymns of praise, experiencing mystical visions (like Paul himself does, as does John the Seer of the Book of Revelation, not to mention mystics such as Teresa of Avila, and so on), dancing (recall King David), or falling into prophetic trances. Our Scriptures are loaded with stories of physically ecstatic experiences such as when Ezekiel is transported by the Spirit to a valley.

If you've had a mystical experience that lasted for any length of time, you probably count it among the most significant spiritual experiences of your life and remain grateful to this day, as you should. Our particular gifts connect us to God personally in profound ways and that is to be enjoyed and relished. How those experiences equip us to be fruitful community members is an important part of integrating such special experiences into our

For Paul, the gift that you have that most builds up the community is the one he considers the "greater" gift; it's not necessarily the one that looks best to the outside world.

communal lives. There are times when our vulnerable sharing of such individual encounters inspires, comforts, and connects us with others or opens new possibilities to those listening. If we pay attention, the context will tell us when such sharing makes for a "we" moment and not just a "me" moment. That's the point the ones speaking in tongues in Corinth were missing.

Maybe you are graced with multiple gifts. That's a wonderful thing to celebrate. For Paul, the gift that you have that most builds up the community is the one he considers the "greater" gift; it's not necessarily the one that looks best to the outside world.

When we come together in a community that includes inquirers and newcomers, we should make sure the gathering serves them well and makes them feel invited to join in. Nothing makes me happier, for instance, than when prospective seminary students visit my class and jump into the discussion. It happens some in the fall semester but more so in the spring as visitors are making their decisions. That means I've been with my class since August and (if all has gone according to plan) we have formed solid, even deep community with inside jokes, shared struggles, and moments of holy transcendence.

I know in advance when prospective students will visit, and I ask the class to (a) help create an inviting, non-cliquish atmosphere and (b) help me "stay in my lane" and act more like I would in the first month with them than the seventh. When we are in spaces with just ourselves and no inquirers, we can "let it all hang out," as it were, and relish that space we have created together over many hours and choices. That space is a gift to be celebrated and to lean on and is an unequivocally good thing (like speaking in tongues). But if we did not adjust our space when visitors join us, it would become a stumbling block. Social context is everything when witnessing to the gospel in living, breathing communities. Here's the litmus test for "mindful Christianity"—can the visitor understand and easily contribute? That's the concern Paul expresses when he asks:

> *What should I do then? I will pray with the spirit, but I will pray with the mind also; I will sing praise with the spirit, but I will sing praise with the mind also. Otherwise, if you say a blessing with the spirit, how can anyone in the position of an outsider say the "Amen" to your thanksgiving, since the outsider does not know what you are saying? For you may give thanks well enough, but the other person is not built up.*
>
> *1 Corinthians 14:15-17*

Do you find your church inviting to visitors or those beyond your congregation? In what ways? What makes you feel welcome (or not) in a Christian gathering?

As it was with idol meat in chapters 8–10, so it is with speaking in tongues—I doubt most of us are losing sleep over it. However, we are back to a very serious issue: how we use our freedom, authority, and gifts. Recall that in chapters 8–10 Paul indicated that he has the freedom and authority to eat whatever he wants based on his advanced knowledge that idols aren't real (and he has the freedom and authority to be paid by the Corinthians, to have a wife, and so on). And recall the power of the "nevertheless" in 9:12b, where he models privileging the needs of the gospel in any given context. Now we see the exact same move. Paul acknowledges that speaking in tongues is a gift and that he has it abundantly (so it's not a case of sour grapes; 14:18). "Nevertheless," he says, "in church I would rather speak five words with my mind, in order to instruct others also, than ten thousand words in a tongue" (14:19).

Paul isn't asking us to pretend that we don't have important gifts and sublime spiritual experiences (that would be false modesty). He also doesn't want us to use those gifts for puffed-up preening purposes (that would be true arrogance). Instead, he invites us to find that sweet spot of "just right" Goldilocks style, which is to own and celebrate our gifts, our spiritual superpowers, to hone them and learn to discern how best to use them in any given situation. That means you may find yourself speaking in tongues in the morning and patently refraining from doing so that same night. Context clues matter. And the greatest context clue is love.

Love (1 Corinthians 13)

Do you remember when we looked at 1 Corinthians 8–10 and noticed that chapter 8 talked about the idol-meat controversy as did chapter 10, but in chapter 9 Paul "went off" on a speech about freedom/authority and his laser sharp "nevertheless"? We learned that chapter 9 was not a digression from the idol-meat controversy—it was the centerpiece. He showed the Corinthians what it looks like to act out of concern for the other, to become all things to all people for the sake of the gospel (not for any other reason—it's not a call to being a doormat or passive in any way).

In chapters 12–14 we have an identical situation. In this unit, in place of the proper use of authority or rights [*exousia*], we have the proper use of gifts. We are faced with the same choice—using it to puff up one's own ego or to build up the common good. Again, chapters 12 and 14 speak directly of spiritual gifts and Paul may seem to "go off" in chapter 13. But chapter 13 is not a digression—it's the centerpiece. One might even argue it's the centerpiece of the Corinthian correspondence or of Paul's theology and ministry as a whole.

Far from being a random separate poem dropped into 1 Corinthians, as some scholars argue, chapter 13 belongs tightly in its literary context.

It begins with the phrase about speaking in tongues because that is the "presenting issue" in this unit and the Corinthian church specifically. Then it moves to prophetic powers, because Paul compares those two in this unit, as we have seen. And he speaks of mysteries in verse 2, which relates directly to 14:2. Throughout Corinthians, we've seen his engagement of "knowledge," which he mentions here in 13:2 also. This chapter was composed to engender real community. Far from a utopian vision or a romantic poem for a wedding, it's the foundational call and shape of Christian community and relationship—all relationship (not just marriage). Notice that while Paul gives very specific advice about prophecy, tongues, and knowledge—that typically prophecy is preferable to tongues and knowledge is good as long as it's chastened by the cross—they will all disappear in the end.

True Christian humility acknowledges that we have only partial knowledge and that we are finite. God-willing, the Corinthians (and we) will put away the childish things and wean off the milk and begin eating solid food, becoming spiritually mature. It is, of course, the spiritually mature who know they know only in part and do not claim too much. They are the ones who have arrived at the knowledge that if they know, it's only because they have been *known*. If they love, it's because God first loved them. I trust you have such folks as mentors and guides on the way and that you serve in that role for others. Though I read 1 Corinthians 13:13 as a Christian and as an NT professor, I never fail to be kind of surprised by it: "And now faith, hope, and love abide, these three; and the greatest of these is love." In some ways, one might expect the "greatest" of these to be faith, given that Paul was an intense evangelist who became "all things to all people, that [he] might by all means save some" (9:22). But in chapter 12, Paul lists faith as a gift, which implies that not everyone will have it, actually. It's not accidental that Paul says that "the greatest of these is love." God is love. We are made in God's image. We came from love, we return to love, we *are* love in our very essence. Love isn't just one of many spiritual gifts.

Do you have favorite quotations on love? Two of mine come from William Sloane Coffin, one-time pastor of Riverside Church:

> Socrates had it wrong; it is not the unexamined but finally the uncommitted life that is not worth living. Descartes too was mistaken; "Cogito ergo sum"—"I think therefore I am"? Nonsense. "Amo ergo sum"—"I love therefore I am." Or, as with unconscious eloquence St. Paul wrote, "Now abide faith, hope, love, these three; and the greatest of these is love."
>
> I believe that. I believe it is better not to live than not to love.[4]
>
> Make love your aim, not biblical inerrancy, nor purity nor obedience to holiness codes. Make love your aim, for
>
>> "Though I speak with the tongues of men and of angels"—musicians, poets, preachers, you are being addressed;
>>
>> "and though I . . . understand all mysteries, and all knowledge"—professors, your turn,
>>
>> "and though I bestow all my goods to feed the poor"—radicals take note;
>>
>> "and though I give my body to be burned"—the very stuff of heroism;
>>
>> "and have not charity, it profiteth me nothing" (1 Cor. 13:1–3 KJV).
>
> I doubt if in any other scriptures of the world there is a more radical statement of ethics. If we fail in love, we fail in all things else.[5]

I routinely read the following passage on the first day of seminary to my students. It's from a collection of letters between a mentor and a college student who is trying to work out her faith and her passion, her gift, her call. In one of his letters, Christopher de Vinck says, "I like your humor and your annoyance at cliché thoughts. . . . No, do not examine your gifts and options and find the best combination that would yield a quality, economically stable job. Examine your passions and pray and light your candles. In many ways, it doesn't matter what you choose. What matters is how you are going to love."[6]

Indeed.

Closing Thoughts

First Corinthians 12–14 gift and grace us with much to dig into as individuals and as a community. I offer the following seven takeaways. What would you add?

1. Everyone has a spiritual gift (or multiple gifts). Everyone.
2. There are no "self-made" people when it comes to gifts. Gifts are given—that's why they're called gifts. They come from God and God alone.
3. No gift is better or worse than another. It's not a competition—it's a symphony.
4. We are all called to discern our gifts, grow them, and use them for the common good. It's crucial to be specific about what gifts we have so that we can own, celebrate, hone, and share our gifts. In the end, here's the point: "To each is given the manifestation of the Spirit for the common good" (1 Corinthians 12:7).
5. We are called to name the gifts of others that we detect in them.
6. In place of domination, we learn that interdependence is the key. With his metaphor of the body, Paul overturns conventional

wisdom (for example, "a head has more honor than a foot") and teaches the ironic Logic of the Cross, where the "apparently" less honored is actually more honored and vice versa.

7. In this chapter we find the repeated themes of interdependence, unity in the Spirit, proper boasting (instead of false modesty or true arrogance), and, ultimately and always, love.

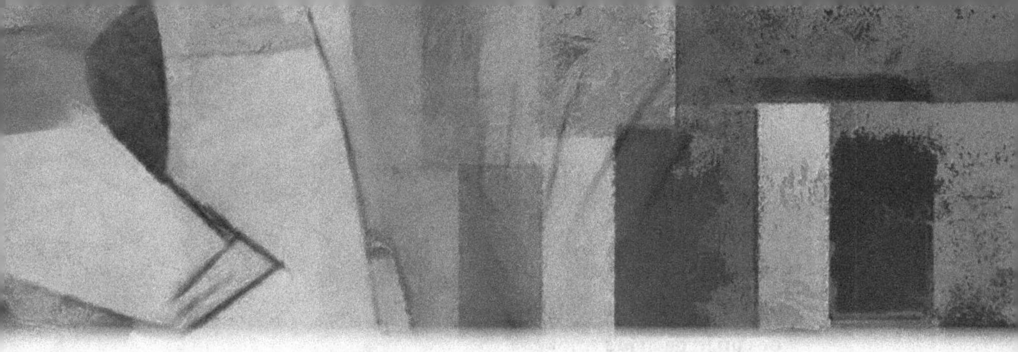

CHAPTER 6

Bodies This Side of the Grave and Beyond (and In Between)

Using a metaphor equating jars and bodies, Paul rightly declares, "We have this treasure in clay jars" (2 Corinthians 4:7). In some ways, we don't just *have* bodies, but we *are* bodies. These bodies regularly attempt to send us information about our well-being. They cause us joy and anxiety and all manner of emotions in between. We have questions about bodies this side of the grave and the other and in between. So, let's spend some time on each.

Bodies feature prominently in 1 Corinthians, as we have noticed. From how we interact with one another sexually (1 Corinthians 5–7) to how our eating choices affect others in private and public settings (1 Corinthians 8–10; 11) to how we clothe our bodies (1 Corinthians 11) to what we do with our tongues (from prophesying to glossolalia to holy kissing; 1 Corinthians 12; 14), our embodied choices convey our values.

So important is the body that Paul uses it as the metaphor for the church—we are the body of Christ. Some are hands, some are feet, but all are of equal importance and no one is more valuable than anyone else. He uses the metaphor again in Romans: "How beautiful are the feet of those who bring good news!" (10:15). We are the body of Christ. As Dorothee Sölle writes in her poem "When he came,"

When he came

He needs you
that's all there is to it
without you he's left hanging
goes up in dachau's smoke
is sugar and spice in the baker's hands
gets revalued in the next stock market crash
he's consumed and blown away
used up
without you

Help him
that's what faith is
he can't bring it about
his kingdom
couldn't then couldn't later can't now
not at any rate without you
and that is his irresistible appeal[1]

Used by permission of Wipf and Stock Publishers. www.wipfandstock.com.

Physical Bodies: Bodies This Side of the Grave (2 Corinthians 4:7-11 and 12:1-10)

In this section, I will address the joys and challenges of embodied existence, ways of thinking about embodied suffering, and how we might be careful to fully include all kinds of bodies in our gathered community, with special attention to people with disabilities (like Paul himself). To do this well, we'll have to look at both 1 and 2 Corinthians, beginning with what Paul says about his physical suffering in 2 Corinthians.

I take it to be a beautiful, if challenging, fact that we have this treasure in clay jars, since the Potter is none other than God Herself. I say Herself here because, in antiquity, women were potters; so when the Old Testament depicts God as a Potter, it's one of the many places that our ancestors depict God in feminized form.[2] God created us as embodied and called it *good.* That's a loaded sentence. Already I hear you both agreeing and pushing back. Those of you currently in the state of falling in love, crushing your PR on your half-marathon, and transporting the rest of us to heavenly heights with your angelic singing voice are saying aloud, "Amen, Jaime!" Those of you spending a majority of your time and money on a body that is failing in one or more ways, those of you caring for someone you love who is slipping away, little by little, whether from dementia or ALS or cancer or addiction may be saying, "Really, Jaime? Embodiment is good?" Yes, embodiment is good. There are numerous ways to understand our bodies.

First, there's the body that gives us a sense of identity. What do you *do* with your body that makes you *you*? Maybe you would answer in one or more of the following ways: I paint; I build; I engineer; I run; I parent; I make people laugh; I help heal other bodies through yoga or massage or physical therapy or surgery; I teach; I tend to people who are dying; I help mend souls; I protect people; I garden/create new life.

Second, there's the body that gives us joy through the experience of the senses. We taste delectable foods and smell our favorite flowers (for me, honeysuckle and jasmine and Texas mountain laurel). We hear children's laughter or music that meets us in our mood or takes us to someplace else we want to go. We see the wonders of the world, whether it's the treasury in Petra or people sharing rather than hoarding resources. We make love, touching and being touched. Each bodily sense can lead us to deeper knowledge about what is true and what is not.

Third, there is the body that suffers. I teach "Evil, Suffering, Death, and the Afterlife in the New Testament," known around campus simply as "the Evil class." It's an important class because the question of suffering, our own and others', can be a deal breaker for many people when it comes to God and faith. At the very least, it raises serious, difficult questions. And it *should,* if you're really paying attention. Léon Bloy once said, "Suffering passes, but the fact of having suffered never passes."[3] It's the topic of the body that suffers that I want us to explore further in this chapter.

The Christian tradition engages suffering head-on. In 2 Corinthians 12:1-10, Paul wrestles with his own physical suffering. After speaking at length about a mystical visionary experience, Paul declares, "To keep me from being too elated, a thorn was given me in the flesh" (12:7). The "was given" is called the "divine passive" and indicates that God did the giving. He also calls the thorn a "messenger of Satan." How can Paul construe an affliction as from *both* God and Satan at the same time? A complex question.

No one knows exactly what Paul's thorny impairment was, but that hasn't stopped anyone from speculating. A speech impediment? Epilepsy? A serious eye malady? Three times—not once, not twice, but three times—Paul "appealed to the Lord about this, that it would leave" him (12:8; compare Jesus praying three times in the Garden of Gethsemane, Mark 14:32-52). Is it right to ask God to relieve our suffering? Absolutely! God replied to Paul, "My grace is sufficient for you, for power is made perfect in weakness" (2 Corinthians 12:9). Now, if we had not been studying 1 Corinthians for five chapters already, we might respond: "Come again? Power is made perfect in weakness? What could that mean?" But we know about the ironic *Logic of the Cross* and the way it redefines wisdom and power, so we are not as shocked when we hear Paul say, "So, I will boast all the more gladly of my weaknesses, so that the power of Christ may dwell in me" (2 Corinthians 12:9).

You signed up for a study on 1 Corinthians, and here I'm drawing you into 2 Corinthians. The reason there is a 2 Corinthians in the canon is because Paul's earlier correspondence with the Corinthians wasn't thoroughly successful. And that's putting it nicely! Throughout the Corinthian correspondence we find "hardship lists" that articulate the types of struggles and suffering Paul experiences as he lives out his earthly journey (for example, 1 Corinthians 4:9-13; 2 Corinthians 4:7-12; 6:4-10). Recall that people

It's not our place to tell someone what their suffering means, but we can certainly accompany them on that journey of discovering or creating meaning.

were questioning Paul's authority for various reasons. One of those is related to this disability thorn. Earlier in the letter, he writes, "For they [that is, the haters, the doubters, the opponents] say, 'His letters are weighty and strong, but *his bodily presence is weak*, and his speech *contemptible*'" (2 Corinthians 10:10, emphasis added). His opponents, some of whom Paul sarcastically calls "superapostles," undermine him and his authority. He never encountered the earthly Jesus like the other apostles did, and, furthermore, he seems to have a so-called "weak" physical presence. SPOILER ALERT: Paul, with all his so-called deficiencies, impairments, and weaknesses, actually makes it into the Christian canon, voluminously.

Paul was doing just fine, better than fine even (Philippians 3:4-6), before he signed on with Jesus. Once he became a follower, however, his struggles began, starting with being struck blind temporarily (according to Acts 9 but never mentioned by Paul himself).

Three "Models" of Suffering

Second Corinthians 12:1-10 displays three different models of suffering that Paul draws upon to locate where God is in the midst of his suffering, to make meaning of his suffering, and to decide how to move forward. When I teach the "Evil" course, I state one goal as, "Let's stop saying stupid stuff about suffering." Not all suffering is the same by any stretch of the imagination. Only the one suffering gets to say, finally, where God is in their experience of suffering. It's not our place to *tell* someone what their suffering *means*, but we can certainly accompany them on that journey of discovering or creating meaning.

In what follows, I draw upon Dr. Susan Garrett's stellar essay, "Paul's Thorn and Cultural Models of Affliction."[4]

Job Model: Affliction as Satanic Test (Job 1:6-12; 2:1-8; Matthew 4:1-11)

In the Job model, the role of Satan as tempter/tester is highlighted. Satan "uses suffering to lead the righteous astray from single-minded commitment to God... by afflicting persons (physically or otherwise) and then offering them an 'easy out.'"[5]

This model employs three assumptions. First, it assumes that human righteousness prompts satanic attacks. This rhetoric appeared with respect to the attacks on the World Trade Center in 2001, with some saying that the tragedy occurred because America is so righteous that Satan had to attack.

Second, the model assumes that the suffering is Satan's contest. Satan serves as an accuser and would like to see Job (and Paul) fail.

Third, the model assumes that Satan and God have an ambiguous relationship. In 2 Corinthians God has given Satan authority to afflict Paul, just as God allows Satan to afflict Job. Satan participates in God's purposes but with nefarious motivations in mind: Satan wants to be able to accuse the afflicted before God for being unable to endure the trial. In the Job model, suffering is negative and prompted by Satan. Read 1 Peter 5:8-9 as another example.

What do Job and Paul teach us about how to respond to this kind of suffering?

First, avoid apostasy when Satan (or whatever your representative of adversity—life, your boss, your ex) afflicts you. Don't chuck faith, don't give in, don't sell out. Put up your dukes and fight (and you might want to learn a few scriptures to verbalize when such trials come [such as 2 Corinthians 4:7-9; Psalm 23; Romans 8:18-30]). Stay in relationship with God, even if it involves cursing the day you were born. Don't use suffering as a reason to bail; rather cling to God all the more.

Second, show compassion to those who suffer. Job's friends did not.

Third, shut up when you don't know what to say. Say, "I don't know what to say, but I'm here with you."

Fourth, understand that you don't have the whole picture (remember, "now we see in a mirror, dimly" [1 Corinthians 13:12]).

Paideia Model: Affliction as Education

Paideia is the Greek word for education; we get the word *pedagogy* (teaching) from it. In this model, the agent of suffering is not Satan, or Satan under the control of God, but rather God alone. Here God is a parent who tests his or her beloved children with suffering in order to chasten or discipline. In this model, suffering is good for us; it teaches us various lessons. It builds character; it corrects; it purifies; it prepares one for accountability (in any aspect of life, whether that be work accountability, health accountability, or accountability on your gospel journey). Think "Coach God." Unlike the Job model, where Satan is the agent of suffering, here it's God. In this model, God may send you texts like my trainer does: "Pain is just weakness leaving the body."

In this model, the appropriate response to suffering is to learn from Coach God. Patient, even athletic endurance is called for. Engage in self-examination. Such endurance is spiritually productive (read Romans 5:3-5; compare 1 Corinthians 11:27-32). I've always been an athlete, and I'm an 8 on the Enneagram. Thus, I almost reflexively embrace this model and find much truth and wisdom in it. I can personally speak to its power and potential.

But this model also raises important questions. How much is enough? If suffering is supposed to "build character" or "teach us a lesson," one has to ask the question of proportion, not to mention logic. If suffering builds character, does that mean we should *add* to someone's suffering to make them a better person instead of seeking to alleviate their suffering? Fuzzy logic in this area increases and concentrates the devastating effects of suffering. Yes, we want to help people develop resilience, absolutely. Run a few extra laps when your quads are burning from being overtaxed and you'll be stronger on the next run. But run on a broken bone and you won't be having a next run. Crushing pain and suffering crushes; it does not strengthen. I want to alert us all to the danger I have seen of buying into what Thomas Tracy calls "a vast pedagogy of pain" as he warns us against carelessly and even fatally lumping all suffering into the "what doesn't kill you makes you stronger" bin.[6] But the gospel patently doesn't condone crushing: "We are afflicted in every way, but not crushed" (2 Corinthians 4:8).

Cross Model

The third model at work in Paul's experience of the thorn in his flesh is what Garrett labels the "cross/resurrection model."[7] The model entails a "lowliness now but exaltation later" approach. We have seen in 1 Corinthians Paul's call to humility, with the Logic of the Cross front and center. The same theme occurs in Jesus's own ministry—"the first will be last" (Matthew 20:16); "The Son of Man came not to be served but to serve" (Matthew 20:28; Mark 10:45); and so on. This is not a call to false modesty or masochism. It's a call to be set free from the ego to live by nothing but the values of God. And since God decided to take on the existence of humanity and Jesus chose the path of humility, that's what actually defines a Christian—moving the ego to the side in order to fully inhabit your true, God-given self, which is always a self in service beyond the self. This is the self that understands it is connected to everything and everyone in God's created order. You are a Good Samaritan called to tend the wounds of someone whom others before you have left on the side of the road to die, literally or figuratively. What's more, God wants us to find meaning in such tending, if not (surprising) joy.

In Paul's own interpretation of his impairment, the thorn helped Paul because he learned that he must humbly depend on God for the strength to endure. Paul actively engages affliction and thereby exhibits strength, but not his *own* strength; rather the site of his affliction becomes the site of

God's manifestation of power, the power of God through the grace of Christ. Notice it is patently *not* the power of "curing" the impairment; rather, it's God's ability to display God's grace and glory through any and every body. Paul shares already (as we can) in the power of the risen Christ. By his logic, if he did not have his affliction, this fact would not be demonstrated. Recall that he was "all that and then some" before his conversion. And as such, he was useless for the gospel. Then he encountered Christ, which according to Acts involved physical blindness, and by his own account he suffered a "thorn in the flesh" that caused others to declare his bodily presence as "weak."

Given this "shameful" disability in a society where men are supposed to carry authority by virile strength, Paul uses logic to show that, despite all odds and biases against him, the gospel was blooming everywhere he stepped, to show that it is God's power acting through Paul. He has a great point! Maybe we should consider chucking the "logic" or "conventional wisdom" of the worlds we inhabit by virtue of our own gender, class, ethnicity, ability, and so on and "pulling a Paul" in our own corner of the world. What would that look like for you?

One caution: Let us not glorify suffering for suffering's sake. Paul only "boasts" about suffering as it relates to his vocational ministry of serving the gospel.

All Diverse Embodiments Make Up the Body of Christ

One area of deep and passionate concern for me is disability. Particularly, I speak and write at length about disability and the Bible and the ways that our texts themselves can be liberating or problematic for people with disabilities, the ways our interpretations of our sacred texts can be liberating or problematic, and the ways our churches can be liberating or problematic. This subject deserves more detailed attention than we can give it here, so I've provided you some further resources to consult at the end of the book. For now, let me offer a few clarifying definitions to help us think about how inclusive we are. We've already raised this question with respect to gender, race, class, and sexuality. One could argue that in our culture being poor, black, lesbian, female, or disabled will make your life more difficult. In addition, "intersectionality" comes into play when an individual embodies a number of categories marginalized by a given society, so how much more marginalized are those who are both black and female or poor and disabled and so on?

Assumptions and Definitions

When entering the conversation about the Bible and disability, a distinction is sometimes made between impairment and disability. A few definitions and comments are in order. First, an *impairment* is a physiological phenomenon located in the body of an individual which may or may not cause pain or discomfort and for which a person may or may not seek a medical cure. An impairment does not necessarily imply a disability (for example, many of us wear glasses for impaired eyes, yet we do not label it a "disability").

Disability is a social phenomenon. A society disables people when it refuses to provide all bodies equal access to the benefits enjoyed by other members of that society, including access to buildings, education, transportation, or political processes. Again, no one thinks twice about having to install lights and pay a light bill for sighted people, thus "accommodating" them (people who are blind don't need the lights). This leads to the question about how a society constructs a notion of the "normate" body, that body that represents the cultural ideals of a given society and by which all bodies are judged as beautiful, valuable, and desirable (or not). It's a construct, and it tells you more about the society itself than any individual in it. What's the "ideal" body in our culture? What color of skin, hair texture and color, eye color, height, weight, freckles or not, age, and so on? How is that "standard" conveyed to us?

Second, "cure" and "healing" are not synonyms. A cure is the removal of a medical impairment and relates to an individual. Healing refers to wholeness and integration of a person with self, the community, and God. Healing may or may not involve a medical cure. Paul never got a cure for the thorn, but he was healed by God's grace (2 Corinthians 12:8-10), whole and integrated with self, the community, and God.

How We Interpret Texts

Sometimes we interpret texts in ways that alienate and burden people with disabilities: for example, anytime we preach or teach in a way that implies that if someone just had more faith, they'd be physically cured. Or we tie sin and suffering together incorrectly, like Job's friends do.[8] Let's get educated for the sake of the gospel. How might such a conversation start regarding the Corinthian correspondence?

1. The Logic of the Cross redefines power and weakness so that, ironically, God has chosen "what is foolish…weak…low and despised in the world" (1 Corinthians 1:27-28). That would generally include women, slaves, and those with physical impairments, like Paul.
2. The fact that one has an impairment (or suffers hardship) does not by definition indicate sin or alienation from God, as Paul's own life shows (not to mention Jesus's).
3. One should feel free to protest one's physical suffering before God and pray for it to cease, as Paul (and Job, and Jesus) demonstrates.
4. The body metaphor and actual bodies remind us that interdependence, not independence, is what God values.

Our Leadership Positions

Not only are people with disabilities to be fully included in the church, ministered to, and considered equally as important as every other person,

Not only are people with disabilities to be fully included in the church, ministered to, and considered equally as important as every other person, but also the church needs to be ministered to by *people with disabilities.*

but also the church needs to be ministered to *by* people with disabilities. If it's true that God has used what is weak in the world to shame the wise and if the least respectable member of the body is more honorable, then those who speak from that place in society, like Paul or the women and slaves who held leadership positions in the ancient church, might have more to teach about wisdom and faith than those the church traditionally raises up or listens to, in direct contradiction to the values of the state.

Our Physical Space

If we truly are inclusive and interdependent, it is imperative that our physical spaces be designed for full participation of all bodies. Can people using wheelchairs access the Communion table, choir loft, and pulpit? Do we have a weird "side door" or "back door" entrance to the sanctuary, or can everyone access it from the front?

Paul helps us notice and solve such obstacles in the Corinthian correspondence.

Mystical Bodies: Bodies This Side of the Grave and Beyond

From Jacob at the River Jabbok in Genesis to John the visionary seeing a new heaven and a new earth in Revelation, not to mention the countless mystics in between and since (like St. Augustine and St. Teresa of Avila, two of the most venerated saints of Christianity), mystical experiences are a rich and valid part of our Christian faith heritage. The Greek word for this state is *ekstasis,* standing outside of (time, space, and so on), being "beside oneself." We get the word *ecstasy* from it. I address this feature of the faith regularly in my teaching, and it typically leads to people wanting to talk to me to explore it further. I'm a little puzzled by the concern people express about their experiences, which they share with me in hushed tones while asking if they are heretics or lunatics based on vivid dreams, encounters with those who have passed on, or other experiences that stand outside of "normal" time and space. People might not be comfortable calling Paul a mystic, but Paul's mystical experiences feature centrally in our faith.

I assume that some readers have had such an experience and some have not. The experience can take numerous forms and lead to different insights. William James way back in 1902 published *The Varieties of Religious Experience,* in which he identified four characteristics of a mystical experience:

1. Ineffability—The individual cannot describe the experience adequately.
2. Noetic quality—The experience leads to knowledge "unplumbed by the discursive intellect" (words like "illumination" or "revelation" or core knowledge are often used) and has "a curious sense of authority for after-time."
3. Transiency—The experience itself does not last long, but the effect can as the person continues to reflect upon the experience and find more meaning and deeper wisdom in the process of reflection.
4. Passivity—Although the individual can encourage a mystical experience by participating in certain activities, like meditation, the state itself is outside the person's own will, and he or she sometimes feels "grasped and held by a superior power."[9]

Let's create spaces of trust where we can discern God speaking into our lives by various means without comparing and contrasting in a competitive way.

Some readers who have experienced the mystical may be able to relate to the language of awe, insight, humility, compassion, and intimacy with God, along with a host of other descriptions. Those who have never had such an experience may doubt the legitimacy of it; I would implore you not to. Just because you yourself have not (yet?) had such an experience does not mean it's not a profound part of our tradition. Perhaps worse, those who have not had such an experience may feel "less than" or "deprived"; I would implore you not to.

God has God's ways of interacting with each of us and none is better than another (just like our spiritual gifts). Let's create spaces of trust where we can discern God speaking into our lives by various means without comparing and contrasting in a competitive way. God has always and will continue to move in mysterious, sometimes mystical ways. How open are you to this? I once spoke to someone about how God appears in dreams, and the person indicated that they would *never* consider dreams a way of God communicating. My response to that is this: If you rule out dreams (or visions, or other people, or ______________ [fill in the blank]), then God patently cannot speak to you that way because even if God tries, you won't honor it; so, by definition God *cannot* speak to you that way.

One challenge in sharing details of a "classical" mystical experience with others, apart from the fact that it's deeply personal and holy ground, is the danger of provoking a kind of "Well, aren't *you* just special" effect upon the audience. But maybe we would feel comfortable sharing experiences "marked by the mystical" or "mystical-*ish*." A few years ago, as part of a structured project, I spent some time reviewing my experience with God from this angle. I was surprised to discover how often the Divine has shown up in unlikely, special, or notable ways that sound kind of crazy when I try to put them into words.

I think of the experience I had in January 1986 as a freshman in college. I was with a group that had rented a church camp for a youth group retreat. I was not there to lead anything but to just be an extra set of hands for a friend. Long story short, I had a vivid encounter with God all alone in the woods, a "come to Jesus" meeting that involved some wrestling and hashing things out and, ultimately, a decision to go ahead and put both feet in with this Christianity thing. After college, I took a youth ministry job at Central Baptist Church in Daytona Beach. In the summer of 1990 we loaded up the youth and headed out to summer camp. Imagine my surprise when the bus turned down the entrance road to the camp and I suddenly realized it was the very place I had had that life-shaping encounter four and a half years earlier.

A few years ago, I was paddleboarding out in the ocean in Florida. I was reflecting on some life lessons to be drawn from paddleboarding out there, including fear and faith (many stories in Scripture about fear and faith are tied to water, such as the "Jesus Stills the Storm" [Matthew 8:23-27; Mark 4:35-41; Luke 8:22-25] and "Jesus Walks on the Water" [Matthew 14:22-33; Mark 6:45-52; John 6:16-21]). For instance, when you see a stingray go beneath your board, you have a tendency to get scared, which causes you to stiffen, which increases the likelihood of falling off of your paddleboard just when that would be least helpful. Same thing when a wave is coming toward you. But if you can breathe, relax, and trust, you will not only stay balanced and afloat, but deeply enjoy the feeling of the moving wave or the beauty of the ray in its natural environment.

I said to God, "This is amazing to be out here all alone in open nature, but you know what would be *really* great? If I got to see *dolphins* (I had been enjoying seeing them from the balcony and from the shore in previous days). I kid you not—within three minutes two dolphins appeared and came within a paddle's length of my board. Admittedly, when I first saw the fins, I had to recall my fear/faith lesson, until I realized they were dolphins and not sharks! I got to enjoy them for a time, chasing them as much as I could to stay near them. It was all grace and joy and restoration and gratitude and intimacy and unity with God and creation. Eventually, they were moving too far out to sea for me to safely follow, and I heard Jesus's words to Peter: "Where I am going, you cannot follow me now; but you *will* follow afterward" (John 13:36, emphasis added). Everything in due time and often in unexpected ways (read the rest of Peter's story and you'll see what I mean).

There was more to the experience as well, but I tell this part in hopes that it jogs your own memory. I would ask you to pause here, really pause, and consider your own faith journey and whether you'd mark any of the experiences along the way as mystical ones, or at least mystical-*ish*. If so, you're not exceptional (sorry) and you're not crazy (you're welcome). I would particularly note that those who have had mystical experiences often report a loss of fear about death and an increased sense of unity with God this side of the grave and beyond.

Spiritual Bodies: Bodies Beyond the Grave (1 Corinthians 15)

What about life beyond the grave? What happens when I die? Where are my loved ones now? Will I recognize my loved ones and be reunited with them? What age will I be in eternity? First Corinthians 15 is the earliest sustained Christian reflection on this question (remember, the Gospels were written after Paul was already dead), so I will focus on the kinds of questions Paul is trying to answer here and how his words relate to questions

modern readers might have about what awaits us beyond our limited space, I will focus on four points (for a de 1 Corinthians 15, read the chapter on Paul in my book *Death and th in the New Testament*).

Death Is Real and Formidable—"The Last Enemy"

The Corinthians, as Greco-Roman Gentiles, held a Platonic notion of immortality instead of resurrection. That is, they believed that the "essential" self was the "naturally" immortal soul and that it was trapped in an annoying, imprisoning body. At death, the soul was released from the body and back to the ether (to eventually inhabit another body). The Greeks even had a phrase for this: *sōma sēma* (the body is a tomb). But from Genesis 1, we know that God chose to create humans and animals and plants and everything else in embodied form and called it "good" rather than "a tomb."

It's not that we are "naturally immortal" and that Jesus died on a cross just so we could get a spiritual body tacked on to an already immortal soul. The Christian message that we get through Paul is much bolder than that: we die. That's why sometimes you feel a hole in your heart and fall down on your knees and scream when someone you love is yanked away by Death. That's a holy reaction and one that God shares. To say that Death is "natural" and pat me on the back while breezily noting that "everything dies—butterflies and people—it's just the circle of life" is to disallow me the chance to rage or have whatever reaction I'm actually having to the real loss of someone I cared about. First Corinthians says that Death is "the last enemy" (15:26). I have capitalized Death here because Paul personifies Death as a force that tries to dig its sharp nails into us, can whisper in our ear, can cackle at our trembling lip.

Death Is Not Ultimate

According to Paul, we will indeed enjoy immortality ("this mortal body *puts on* immortality" [1 Corinthians 15:54, emphasis added]), but it's a hard-won immortality through the death and resurrection of Jesus. Christianity is a resurrection faith. Resurrection takes death seriously; Platonism does not. Resurrection says Death is real, not an illusion. Death is sad and painful—even the best deaths. Death may dog us, try to drag us down into hopelessness and loneliness and fear, *and yet* it does not have the last word, its days are numbered, and its defeat is sure: "When this perishable body puts on imperishability, and this mortal body puts on immortality, then the saying that is written will be fulfilled: / 'Death has been swallowed up in victory'" (1 Corinthians 15:54). Our biblical canon is set up to remind us that we live in a time between the perfect beginning (Genesis) and the glorious ending (Revelation), and Paul is a master of helping us navigate this time with honesty, courage, and hope.

God Wins—Completely

Jesus vanquished Death and proved that God is always in the business of life and re-creation, now and forever. Reread 1 Corinthians 15:24-28, where Paul insists that when all is said and done, God will be "all in all" or "everything to everyone" [Gk. *panta en pasin*]. It is not surprising then, that you will find no language of hell in Paul's writings, since such a notion would imply there is a place or state of being where God is *not* all in all or everything to everyone. It wouldn't make any sense. The cross shows the victory of the greatest of these: *love*. Jesus did not go to the cross for God to be "most things to most people" any more than God will ever stop leaving the ninety-nine to go in search of the one. This is the same Paul who tells us in Romans 3:3-4 that God's faithfulness is more powerful than our faithlessness: "What if some were unfaithful? Will their faithlessness nullify the faithfulness of God? By no means!"

Embodiment Is Still Good, Eternally

The Corinthians want to know what kind of body we will have beyond the grave (1 Corinthians 15:35). Paul offers an argument, the crux of which is this: "Trust God (to supply you with whatever kind of body is appropriate or relevant for eternity)." Paul reminds them that God has given stars star bodies and animals animal bodies and so on. Stop fretting. God knows what God is doing.

Side note: Christians should consider being organ donors. I say this because this is a serious concern for some Christians, and they take perfectly good organs with them to the grave. While I would never denigrate someone's faithful concern, I want to be clear that Scripture gives no reason to make such a decision. God doesn't need your earthly liver in the afterlife to outfit you with your "spiritual body." If God can create the world and everything in it in the first place, trust God to be able to do so always and everywhere. Save the life on earth of that person whom God also created and loves. Related to that, some Christians wonder if cremation is a faithful option. Indeed it is, for the same reasons just noted. Trust God's creative ability.

The Redemption of *All* Creation

The final defeat of Death and attainment of perfect unity with God includes all of creation, not just humans. Again, God has always tended to all of creation (1 Corinthians 15:39-41; consult also Romans 8:18-23; Genesis 1–2). Those Christian denominations that do the Blessing of the Animals services "get it" when it comes to this.

But What About _____?

Often, many questions arise that space does not permit treating here, but I want to address a few. First, people ask about their personal identity in the afterlife. Will I be me? This gets into larger existential questions. If I were to look at photos of you from birth until right now, which one is "really" you? Six months old? Ten years old? Sixty? They are all "you." While the subject may be interesting to ponder, the main point again is that God created you, knows you, and, as one song puts it, "God is madly in love with you"![10] Trust God to take care of the details.

Second, will there be "special relationships" beyond the grave? Will you be in relationship with your current partner, for example? Again, this is a vast topic. It's worth asking about. If I were there with you, I'd talk about agape love, which never dies but always expands to include more and more in its embrace. If Paul (and John, among others) is correct and God is love and the greatest of these is love, then it makes sense that when we no longer see through a mirror dimly, but face to face, we'll have the blinders, which keep us trained only on those who matter most to us now, taken off and experience God's own view—a scope large enough to love all. In addition, if Paul believes that in Christ there is no longer Jew nor Greek, slave nor free, male and female, what does this mean for such identity markers in the eschaton? Jesus says there will be no marriage in heaven, but we will be "like angels" (Matthew 22:30). This gets into the subject of what the afterlife could entail.

Finally, what about the fact that not all Christians share the same beliefs about bodies beyond the grave? Even the biblical authors didn't share the exact same beliefs. It doesn't make you "not a Christian" if you believe one thing but not another, despite what someone might say to you. In fact, what first got me interested in discovering what the Bible says about it was my work at hospice. I had no idea that people who all call themselves Christian had such varying beliefs about what was happening in the present and what the afterlife entails. If the biblical authors can have different understandings, then we can question them and each other as we seek truth. God surely delights in our investigations and conversations, and we are always reminded that now we know "only in part," as Paul himself admits (1 Corinthians 13:12). He's putting forth the best argument he has based on what he knows in the moment, drawing upon reason (though we might take issue with some of his reasoning), tradition, Scripture, and experience. We are surely called to do the same now with the help of the Holy Spirit.

Closing Thoughts

In the end, 1 Corinthians insists on hope and gospel and trust in God as creator, redeemer, and sustainer. As Paul will say later, in Romans 14:8-9, "If we live, we live to the Lord, and if we die, we die to the Lord; so then, whether we live or whether we die, we are the Lord's. For to this end Christ died and lived again, so that he might be Lord of both the dead and the living." Trying to wrangle over details beyond that is probably not very productive.

Because we know that we are God's this side of the grave and beyond, we can live and die with abandon for the sake of love, letting go of anxieties about the exact details. There's a freedom in letting go and living in accordance with who we are called to be right here and now. And by the way, since we know we will die and we know what we value most, why not consider writing an "ethical will" to pass on to those behind us? We have a will for stuff, but how about a will in which you pass on the most important values and life lessons you've collected? Then you will say, like Paul in 1 Corinthians 15:3, "I handed on to you as of first importance what I in turn had received."

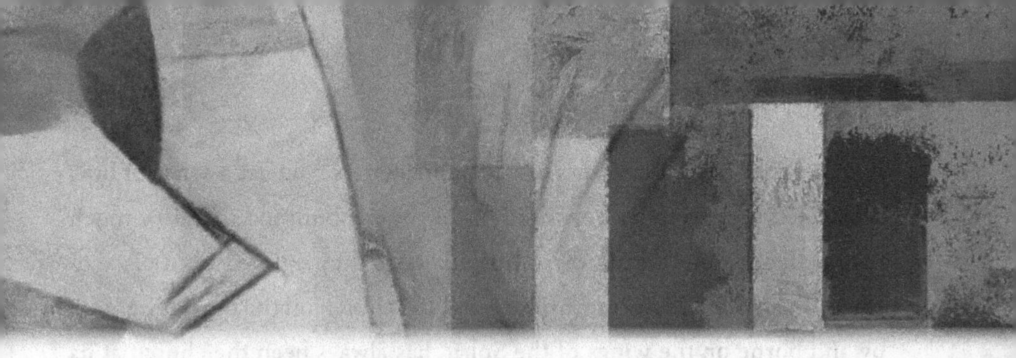

CONCLUSION

Ending with Love (1 Corinthians 16)

On the Road Again...

As Paul's letter to the Corinthians comes to an end, so does this book. Reading the endings of Pauline letters can be fascinating because they are filled with details that remind us these are written by a real, historical person to a real, historical, specific group of people. We hear about a slew of other individuals and groups we meet in his other letters (many of which he has already written by the time he writes 1 Corinthians). You get a strong sense of the energy and vitality of the mission. He refers to his relationship with the churches in Galatia and his travel plans to stay in Ephesus (whence he is writing the letter) and then visit them in Corinth after passing through Macedonia. We see Timothy and Apollos perhaps going to Corinth soon as well.

We recall that Stephanas and Fortunatus and Achaicus are in Ephesus, having come from the Corinthian church. Prisca and Aquila are also in Ephesus with Paul at the moment, though they eventually go back to Rome, as we know from Romans 16:3-5. The saying "all roads lead to Rome" was largely true at this time, and Christians took advantage of the Roman road system to make a living and spread the gospel, wherever life and work took them.

If you read these last chapters of all Pauline letters, you get a sense of how connected they were far beyond their own neighborhood and how much they depended on one another's hospitality as they traveled from place to place. The mobility is astonishing, really. The church on the move, swept up by and borne on the wings of the Spirit, has always been the church at its most life-giving and transformational.

The Jerusalem Collection: Celebrating Unity within Diversity

Another item to highlight is the importance of collecting money for the poor in Jerusalem with which 1 Corinthians 16 begins. If you read Galatians 1:11–2:14, you'll see Paul clarifying how his Gentile mission relates to the largely Jewish mission of James, John, and Peter (called Cephas there). You'll also notice tension around that meeting in Jerusalem, not to mention Paul getting in Peter's face. To put it simply, they agreed that though they had unity in Christ, the shape and specifics of their missions were not identical—Paul was called to the Gentiles (the uncircumcised) and they to Jews (the circumcised). At Galatians 2:10 we read: "They [the Jerusalem leaders] asked only one thing, that we remember the poor, which was actually what I was eager to do." Thus, we call this "the Jerusalem Collection," and you will see reference to it in multiple Pauline letters.

The symbolic importance of the collection was to show unity within diversity. The two missions looked different in terms of ethnic culture and practices (foods eaten, circumcision, and so on), but the unity was found in the fact that Christ died and was raised for all; God shows no partiality. They didn't have to agree on many of the details in order to go get God's work done! I find that fact compelling. We can stop wasting time with internal Christian debate, agree to disagree, and go be about God's business of good news.

Go be about God's business of good news.

Kisses and Hugs

Like Paul, we begin and end with the Logic of the Cross, which is shorthand for the Logic of Love. When we "search the depths of God," no matter where or how we start our search, we will always end up at the same place: love. The paradox of a crucified Messiah has taught us to redefine categories like weakness vs. power and wisdom vs. foolishness. Following this Messiah shapes our lives in very particular ways; it dictates our life purpose and therefore our ethics. On our best days, it makes us eager to "become all things to all people" that we might participate in God's saving, healing work, eager to "do it all for the sake of the gospel" (1 Corinthians 9:22-23). We relax into and celebrate our unity in Christ and diversity in gifts, embodiments, and ministries. We rejoice in the knowledge that we are part of a resurrection faith that overcomes death in all in its forms:

> *Thanks be to God, who gives us the victory through our Lord Jesus Christ.*
>
> *Therefore, my beloved, be steadfast, immovable, always excelling in the work of the Lord, because you know that in the Lord your labor is not in vain.*
>
> *1 Corinthians 15:57-58*

Friends, we have journeyed with Paul and the Corinthians. As Paul calls us to "greet one another with a holy kiss" (16:20), consider yourself holy-kissed from Dallas. After all we've learned, we are not surprised that Paul concludes the letter with love, and I do the same with this book:

> *The grace of the Lord Jesus be with you. My love be with all of you in Christ Jesus.*
>
> *1 Corinthians 16:23-24*

Further Resources

Augustine. *Homilies on the First Epistle of John.* In *A Select Library of the Nicene and Post-Nicene Fathers of the Christian Church.* First Series, vol. 7, edited by Philip Schaff. Translated by H. Browne. Revised by Joseph H. Myers. New York: Christian Literature Company, 1888.

Black, Kathy. *A Healing Homiletic: Preaching and Disability.* Nashville, TN: Abingdon Press, 1996.

Brach, Tara. *Radical Compassion: Learning to Love Yourself and Your World with the Practice of RAIN.* New York: Viking, 2019.

Buckingham, Marcus, and Donald O. Clifton. *Now, Discover Your Strengths.* New York: The Free Press, 2001.

Buechner, Frederick. *Peculiar Treasures: A Biblical Who's Who.* San Francisco: HarperSanFrancisco, 1979.

Clark-Soles, Jaime. *Death and the Afterlife in the New Testament.* New York: T&T Clark, 2006.

Clark-Soles, Jaime. "Johannine Literature: John, First–Third John, and Revelation." Chap. 10 in *The Bible and Disability: A Commentary,* edited by Sarah J. Melcher, Mikeal C. Parsons, and Amos Yong. Waco, TX: Baylor University Press, 2017.

Clark-Soles, Jaime. "More than Conquerors: Romans 8:26–39 and Disability." HuffPost, updated September 20, 2014. https://www.huffpost.com/entry/more-than-conquerors_b_5607078.

Clark-Soles, Jaime. "The Afterlife: Considering Heaven and Hell." *Word and World* 31, no. 1 (Winter 2011): 65–74.

Clark-Soles, Jaime. "Women in Paul's Ministry." Chap. 9: in *Women in the Bible*. Interpretation: Resources for the Use of Scripture in the Church. Louisville, KY: Westminster John Knox, 2020.

Coffin, William Sloane. *Credo*. Louisville, KY: Westminster John Knox Press, 2004.

de Vinck, Christopher, and Elizabeth M. Mosbo VerHage. *Compelled to Write to You: Letters on Faith, Love, Service, and Life*. Nashville, TN: Upper Room, 2001.

Dickinson, Emily. "Tell all the truth but tell it slant—" (1263). In *The Poems of Emily Dickinson: Reading Edition,* edited by Ralph W. Franklin. Cambridge, MA: The Belknap Press, 1998.

Eisenbaum, Pamela. *Paul Was Not a Christian: The Original Message of a Misunderstood Apostle*. New York: HarperOne, 2009.

Garrett, Susan R. "Paul's Thorn and Cultural Models of Affliction." Chap. 6 in *The Social World of the First Christians: Essays in Honor of Wayne A. Meeks,* edited by L. Michael White and O. Larry Yarbrough. Minneapolis, MN: Fortress Press, 1995.

Guest, Deryn, Robert E. Goss, Mona West, and Thomas Bohache, eds., *The Queer Bible Commentary*. London: SCM Press, 2011.

Hillsong UNITED. "Good Grace," by Joel Houston. Copyright © 2018 Hillsong MP Songs (BMI) (adm. in the US and Canada at CapitolCMGPublishing.com) All rights reserved. Track 19 on *People* (Live). Capitol Christian Music Group / Sparrow Records, 2019.

James, William. *The Varieties of Religious Experience: A Study in Human Nature,* edited by Martin E. Marty. New York: Penguin Group, 1982. First published in the United States of America by Longmans, Green, and Co., 1902.

Johansen, Bob. *The New Leadership Literacies: Thriving in a Future of Extreme Disruption and Distributed Everything*. Oakland, CA: Berrett-Koehler, 2017.

Kornfield, Jack. "Seeing the Goodness in Another Being," YouTube video, 2:39, posted on Jack Kornfield channel, May 24, 2019. https://www.youtube.com/watch?v=0F2CF4Jc2mg.

Martin, Dale B. *The Corinthian Body*. New Haven, CT: Yale University Press, 1995.

Meeks, Wayne A. *The First Urban Christians: The Social World of the Apostle Paul*, 2nd ed. New Haven, CT: Yale University Press, 2003.

Melcher, Sarah J., Mikeal C. Parsons, and Amos Yong, eds. *The Bible and Disability: A Commentary*. Waco, TX: Baylor University Press, 2017.

Metzger, Bruce M., and Bart D. Ehrman. *The Text of the New Testament: Its Transmission, Corruption, and Restoration*, 4th ed. New York: Oxford University Press, 2005.

Miles, Sara. *Take This Bread: A Radical Conversion*. New York: Ballantine Books, 2008.

Sölle, Dorothee. "When he came." In *Revolutionary Patience*, 7–17. Eugene, OR: Wipf and Stock Publishers, 2003. Previously published 1974 by Orbis Books.

Thoet, Alison. "'It's a Potluck Dinner Versus the Melting Pot': 6 Books for Appreciating Other Religions," PBS News Hour, September 12, 2018. https://www.pbs.org/newshour/nation/its-a-potluck-dinner-versus-the-melting-pot-6-books-for-appreciating-other-religions.

Tracy, Thomas F. "Why Do the Innocent Suffer?" Chap. 3 in *Why Are We Here? Everyday Questions and the Christian Life*, edited by Ronald F. Thiemann and William C. Placher, 40–55. Harrisburg, PA: Trinity Press International, 1998.

Williamson, Marianne. *A Return to Love: Reflections on the Principles of A Course in Miracles*. New York: HarperCollins, 1996.

Wingfield, Mark. *Why Churches Need to Talk about Sexuality: Lessons Learned from Hard Conversations about Sex, Gender, Identity, and the Bible*. Minneapolis, MN: Fortress Press, 2019.

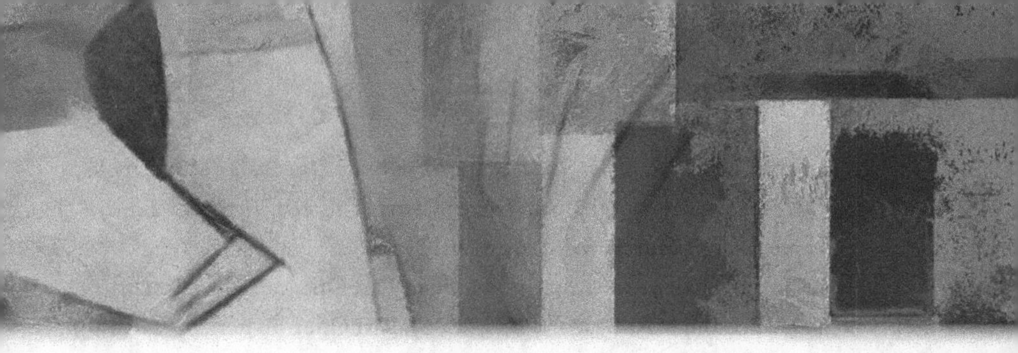

Notes

INTRODUCTION

1 Alison Thoet, "'It's a Potluck Dinner Versus the Melting Pot': 6 Books for Appreciating Other Religions," PBS News Hour, September 12, 2018, https://www.pbs.org/newshour/nation/its-a-potluck-dinner-versus-the-melting-pot-6-books-for-appreciating-other-religions.

2 Emily Dickinson talks about telling the truth with a slant (the whole truth but somehow not exactly straight) in her poem, "Tell all the truth but tell it slant—" (1263), in *The Poems of Emily Dickinson: Reading Edition*, ed. Ralph W. Franklin (Cambridge, MA: The Belknap Press, 1998).

CHAPTER 1:
Can't We All Just Get Along?

1 Frederick Buechner, *Peculiar Treasures: A Biblical Who's Who* (San Francisco: HarperSanFrancisco, 1979), 146.

2 Marianne Williamson, *A Return to Love: Reflections on the Principles of A Course in Miracles* (New York: HarperCollins, 1996), 190–191. The quotation contains Williamson's paraphrased interpretations (denoted by single quotation marks) of *A Course in Miracles*, copyright 1975, Foundation for Inner Peace, Inc.

CHAPTER 2:
Relationship Status: It's Complicated

1 For those who want more knowledge, I recommend Mark Wingfield, *Why Churches Need to Talk about Sexuality: Lessons Learned from*

Hard Conversations about Sex, Gender, Identity, and the Bible (Minneapolis, MN: Fortress Press, 2019) and Deryn Guest et al., eds, *The Queer Bible Commentary* (London: SCM Press, 2011).

2 Viktor E. Frankl, *Man's Search for Meaning*, Part One trans. Ilse Lasch (1959; Boston, MA: Beacon Press, 2006), Part One: "Experiences in a Concentration Camp," 66.

CHAPTER 3:
Freedom: From What, For What?

1 Augustine, *Homilies on the First Epistle of John*, vol. 7 of *A Select Library of the Nicene and Post-Nicene Fathers of the Christian Church*, First Series, ed. Philip Schaff, trans. H. Browne, revised by Joseph H. Myers (New York: Christian Literature Company, 1888), 504.

2 Bob Johansen, *The New Leadership Literacies: Thriving in a Future of Extreme Disruption and Distributed Everything* (Oakland, CA: Berrett-Koehler, 2017), x.

3 Johansen, *The New Leadership Literacies*, 1.

4 Johansen, 19.

5 Johansen, 129.

6 Tara Brach, *Radical Compassion: Learning to Love Yourself and Your World with the Practice of RAIN* (New York: Viking, 2019), xxii.

CHAPTER 4:
Gathering for Good

1 Jaime Clark-Soles, chap. 9: "Women in Paul's Ministry," in *Women in the Bible*, Interpretation: Resources for the Use of Scripture in the Church (Louisville, KY: Westminster John Knox, 2020).

2 If you want to know more, read chap. 9: "Prophylactic Veils" on 1 Corinthians 11 in Dale B. Martin, *The Corinthian Body* (New Haven, CT: Yale University Press, 1995), 229–249.

3 Wayne A. Meeks, *The First Urban Christians: The Social World of the Apostle Paul*, 2nd ed. (New Haven, CT: Yale University Press, 2003), 70.

4 Clark-Soles, "Women in Paul's Ministry."

5 Clark-Soles, "Women in Paul's Ministry."
6 Clark-Soles, "Women in Paul's Ministry."
7 Originally published in Jennifer Logsdon-Kellogg, "The Body of Christ Given—," *2014-2015 Perkins School of Theology Student Journal* 14 (Fall 2014), 83–84.
8 Logsdon-Kellogg, "The Body of Christ Given—," *Student Journal*, p. 85.
9 Sara Miles, *Take This Bread: A Radical Conversion* (New York: Ballantine Books, 2008), 57–58.

CHAPTER 5:
Talented and Gifted

1 Jack Kornfield, "Seeing the Goodness in Another Being," YouTube video, 2:39, posted on Jack Kornfield channel, May 24, 2019, https://www.youtube.com/watch?v=0F2CF4Jc2mg.
2 Marcus Buckingham and Donald O. Clifton, *Now, Discover Your Strengths* (New York: The Free Press, 2001), 7.
3 Buckingham and Clifton, *Now, Discover Your Strengths*, 8.
4 William Sloane Coffin, *Credo* (Louisville, KY: Westminster John Knox Press, 2004), 5.
5 Coffin, *Credo*, 5–6.
6 Christopher de Vinck and Elizabeth M. Mosbo VerHage, *Compelled to Write to You: Letters on Faith, Love, Service, and Life* (Nashville, TN: Upper Room, 2001), 64.

CHAPTER 6:
Bodies This Side of the Grave and Beyond (and In Between)

1 Dorothee Sölle, "When he came," in *Revolutionary Patience* (Eugene, OR: Wipf and Stock Publishers, 2003), 7.
2 For more on this topic, see Jaime Clark-Soles, chap. 2: "God across Gender," in *Women in the Bible*.
3 Léon Bloy, quoted in F. J. J. Buytendijk, *Pain: Its Modes and Functions*, trans. Eda O'Shiel (Chicago, IL: University of Chicago Press, 1962), 20.

4 Susan R. Garrett, chap. 6: "Paul's Thorn and Cultural Models of Affliction," in *The Social World of the First Christians: Essays in Honor of Wayne A. Meeks*, ed. L. Michael White and O. Larry Yarbrough (Minneapolis, MN: Fortress Press, 1995), 82–99.

5 Garrett, "Paul's Thorn," 87.

6 Thomas F. Tracy, chap. 3: "Why Do the Innocent Suffer?," in *Why Are We Here? Everyday Questions and the Christian Life*, ed. Ronald F. Thiemann and William C. Placher (Harrisburg, PA: Trinity Press International, 1998), 49–51.

7 Garrett, "Paul's Thorn," 94.

8 There are many resources now to help us interpret with more care, such as Kathy Black, *A Healing Homiletic: Preaching and Disability* (Nashville, TN: Abingdon, 1996); and Sarah J. Melcher, Mikeal C. Parsons, and Amos Yong, eds., *The Bible and Disability: A Commentary* (Waco, TX: Baylor University Press, 2017).

9 William James, *The Varieties of Religious Experience: A Study in Human Nature*, ed. Martin E. Marty (New York: Penguin Group, 1982), 380–382.

10 Hillsong UNITED, "Good Grace," by Joel Houston, track 19 on *People* (Live), 2019.

Printed in the USA
CPSIA information can be obtained
at www.ICGtesting.com
JSHW030436040124
54765JS00007B/224